LEONARD ROY FRANK

Quotes and Passages From the World's Greatest Freethinkers

freedom

RANDOM HOUSE
REFERENCE

This book is available for special purchases in bulk by organizations and institutions, not for resale, at special discounts. Please direct your inquiries to Random House Premium Sales, fax 212-572-4961.

Please address inquiries about electronic licensing of reference products, for use on a network or in software or on CD-ROM, to the Subsidiary Rights Department, Random House Reference, fax 212-940-7352.

Visit the Random House Reference Web site at www.randomwords.com

Typeset and printed in the United States of America

DESIGN BY ELINA D. NUDELMAN

Library of Congress Cataloging-in-Publication Data is available

0 9 8 7 6 5 4 3 2 1

ISBN: 0-375-42585-3

contents

introduction

Why a book about freedom? Because freedom is a critical factor in our lives, because there is little agreement on what exactly constitutes freedom, and because freedom is a solid measure of individual and social progress.

To clarify and stimulate thought on freedom, I have culled more than six-hundred passages and quotations from four decades of reading and study. They are drawn from essays, interviews, letters, plays, novels, poems, songs, as well as from speeches, political documents, and legal opinions. My intention is to bring together the best ideas from as diverse a group of people as possible: all colors and backgrounds, artists and activists, philosophers and historians, political leaders and judges, the famous and the unknown.

The thirty-three alphabetically arranged themes include conscience, democracy, equality, free will and destiny, freedom defended, freedom's struggle, independence, the individual, justice, law, the mind, the press, responsibility, self-realization, social change and speech.

Each entry consists of a quotation followed by its author (or source) and typically the author's nationality, profession, and birth and death years, except with living authors in which case the word "contemporary" replaces the years. An Authors Index in the back of the book lists the page number for each entry.

At this time of unprecedented opportunity and danger, our heritage of freedom has never seemed more important. Although reality hasn't always matched the words of freedom's champions, we must grant that these words may yet serve as beacons along the pathway to a freer tomorrow, one in which all of the earth's creatures may live together in harmony. With trust, courage and resolve, it is surely in our power to bring this to pass.

AMERICA
america

I pledge allegiance to the flag of the United States of America and to the republic for which it stands, one nation under God, indivisible, with liberty and justice for all.

FRANCIS BELLAMY (U.S. clergyman, 1856–1931),
"The Pledge of Allegiance"

The American Creed affirms those truths our founders held self-evident: **JUSTICE FOR ALL, BECAUSE WE ARE ALL CREATED EQUAL; AND LIBERTY FOR ALL, BECAUSE WE ARE ALL ENDOWED BY THE CREATOR WITH CERTAIN INALIENABLE RIGHTS.** America's fidelity to this creed is judged by history. Living up to it remains a constant challenge. But it invests our nation with spiritual purpose and—if we honor its precepts—a moral destiny.

FORREST CHURCH (contemporary
U.S. clergyman and writer)

We, the people of the United States, in order to form a more perfect union, establish justice, insure domestic tranquility, provide for the common defense, promote the general welfare, and secure the blessings of liberty to ourselves and our posterity, do ordain and establish this Constitution for the United States of America.

CONSTITUTION OF THE UNITED STATES, Preamble, 1787

America is best described by one word, **FREEDOM.**

DWIGHT D. EISENHOWER (U.S. president, 1890–1969)

To make good the cause of Freedom against Slavery you must be . . . Declarations of Independence walking.

RALPH WALDO EMERSON (U.S. philosopher, 1803–1882)

DECLARATION OF INDEPENDENCE

When, in the course of human events, it becomes necessary for one people to dissolve the political bands which have connected them with another, and to assume, among the powers of the earth, the separate and equal station to which the laws of nature and of nature's God entitle them, a decent respect to the opinions of mankind requires that they should declare the cause which impel them to the separation.

We hold these truths to be self-evident, that all men are created equal, that they are endowed by their Creator with certain unalienable rights, that among these are life, liberty, and the pursuit of happiness. That, to secure these rights, governments are instituted among men, deriving their just powers from the consent of the governed. That, whenever any form of government becomes destructive of these ends, it is the right of the people to alter or to abolish it, and to institute new government, laying its foundation on such principles, and organizing its power in such form, as to them shall seem most likely to affect their safety and happiness. . . .

The history of the present King of Great Britain is a history of repeated injuries and usurpations, all having in direct object the establishment of an absolute tyranny over these states. [At this point, twenty-seven specific grievances against the king are listed.]

We, therefore, the representatives of the United States of America, in General Congress assembled, appealing to the Supreme Judge of the world for the rectitude of our intentions, do, in the name, and by authority of the good people of these colonies, solemnly publish and declare, that these United Colonies are, and of right ought to be free and independent states; that they are absolved from all allegiance to the British Crown, and that all political connection between them and the state of Great Britain is and ought to be totally dissolved; and that, as free and independent states, they have full power to levy war, conclude peace, contract alliances, establish commerce, and to do all other acts and things which independent states may of right do. And for the support of this declaration, with a firm reliance on the protection of divine Providence, we mutually pledge to each other our lives, our fortunes, and our sacred honor.

THOMAS JEFFERSON (U.S. president, 1743–1826), July 4, 1776

It is not our affluence, or our plumbing, or our clogged freeways that grip the imagination of others. Rather, it is the values upon which our system is built. These values imply our adherence not only to liberty and individual freedom, but also to international peace, law and order, and constructive social purpose. When we depart from these values, we do so at our peril.

J. WILLIAM FULBRIGHT (Arkansas senator,
1905–1995)

Our Constitution is color-blind, and neither knows nor tolerates classes among citizens. In respect of civil rights, all citizens are equal before the law. The humblest is the peer of the most powerful.

JOHN MARSHALL HARLAN (U.S. Supreme Court
associate justice, 1833–1911)

IT IS POSSIBLE TO READ THE HISTORY OF THIS COUN-TRY AS ONE LONG STRUGGLE TO EXTEND THE LIBER-TIES ESTABLISHED IN OUR CONSTITUTION TO EVERY-ONE IN AMERICA.

MOLLY IVINS (contemporary U.S. journalist)

The last hope of human liberty in this world rests on us.

THOMAS JEFFERSON

And so, my fellow Americans: ask not what your country can do for you-ask what you can do for your country. My fellow citizens of the world: ask not what America will do for you, but what together we can do for the freedom of man.

JOHN F. KENNEDY (U.S. president, 1917–1963),
Inaugural Address, January 20, 1961

Give me your tired, your poor,
Your huddled masses yearning to breathe free.
The wretched refuse of your teeming shore,
Send these, the homeless, tempest-tossed, to me:
I lift my lamp beside the golden door.

EMMA LAZARUS (U.S. poet, 1849–1887), "The New Colossus." The poem was inscribed at the foot of the Statute of Liberty in New York harbor in 1886.

GETTYSBURG ADDRESS

Forescore and seven years ago our fathers brought forth on this continent; a new nation, conceived in liberty, and dedicated to the proposition that all men are created equal.

Now we are engaged in a great civil war, testing whether that nation, or any nation so conceived and so dedicated, can long endure. We are met on a great battlefield of that war. We have come to dedicate a portion of that field, as a final resting place for those who here gave their lives that that nation might live. It is altogether fitting and proper that we should do this.

But, in a larger sense, we can not dedicate—we cannot consecrate—we cannot hallow-this ground. The brave men, living and dead, who struggled here, have consecrated it, far above our poor power to add or detract. The world will little note, nor long remember what we say here, but it can never forget what they did here.

It is for us the living, rather, to be dedicated here to the unfinished work which they who fought here have thus far so nobly advanced. It is rather for us to be here dedicated to the great task remaining before us—that from these honored dead we take increased devotion to that cause for which they gave the last full measure of devotion—that we here highly resolve that these dead shall not have died in vain—that this nation, under God, shall have a new birth of freedom—and that government of the people, by the people, for the people, shall not perish from the earth.

ABRAHAM LINCOLN (U.S. president, 1809–1865) Gettysburg Address, November 19, 1863. In 1950, soon after the Soviet Union began the Berlin Blockade, the American people gave the people of that city a Liberty Bell that was placed in West Berlin's Schöneberg City Hall. The inscription on the bell read, "That this world, under God, shall have a new birth of freedom."

It was not the mere matter of the separation of the colonies from the motherland; but something in the Declaration giving liberty, not alone to the people of this country, but hope to the world for all future time. It was that which gave promise that in due time the weights should be lifted from the shoulders of all men, and that all should have an equal chance. This is the sentiment embodied in that Declaration of Independence.

ABRAHAM LINCOLN, Independence Hall speech, Philadelphia, February 22, 1861, en route to Washington, D.C. to assume the presidency

We have it in our power to begin the world over again. A situation, similar to the present, hath not happened since the days of Noah until now. The birthday of a new world is at hand, and a race of man . . . are to receive their portion of freedom from the event of a few months.

THOMAS PAINE (English-born U.S. political philosopher, 1737–1809), *Common Sense,* 1776

There is what I call the American idea. . . . This idea demands, as the proximate organization thereof, a democracy; that is, a government of all the people, by all the people, for all the people; of course, a government of the principles of eternal justice, the unchanging law of God: **FOR SHORTNESS' SAKE I WILL CALL IT THE IDEA OF FREEDOM.**

THEODORE PARKER (U.S. clergyman and social reformer, 1810–1860)

In one generation we have moved from denying a black man service at a lunch counter to elevating one to the highest military office in the nation, and to being a serious contender for the presidency.

This is a magnificent country and I am proud to be one of its sons.

COLIN L. POWELL (contemporary U.S. secretary of state), announcing his decision not to seek the presidency, 1995

THE "FOUR FREEDOMS" SPEECH

IN THE FUTURE DAYS, WHICH WE SEEK TO MAKE SECURE, WE LOOK FORWARD TO A WORLD FOUNDED UPON FOUR ESSENTIAL HUMAN FREEDOMS.

THE FIRST IS FREEDOM OF SPEECH AND EXPRESSION—everywhere in the world.

THE SECOND IS FREEDOM OF EVERY PERSON TO WORSHIP GOD IN HIS OWN WAY—everywhere in the world.

THE THIRD IS FREEDOM FROM WANT—which, translated into world terms, means economic understandings which will secure to every nation a healthy peacetime life for its inhabitants—everywhere in the world.

THE FOURTH IS FREEDOM FROM FEAR—which, translated into world terms, means a world-wide reduction of armaments to such a point and in such a thorough fashion that no nation will be in a position to commit an act of physical aggression against any neighbor—anywhere in the world.

That is no vision of a distant millennium. It is a definite basis for a kind of world attainable in our own time and generation.

FRANKLIN D. ROOSEVELT (U.S. president, 1882–1945), Message to Congress, January 6, 1941

There's a tendency to throw aside old values as belonging to an earlier generation. Don't discard those values that have proven, over the period of time, their value. Just believe in those values that made our nation great and keep them: faith, family, hard work, and, above all, freedom.

RONALD REAGAN (contemporary U.S. president)

The preservation of the sacred fire of liberty, and the destiny of its republican model of government are justly considered, perhaps as deeply, as finally, staked on the experiment entrusted to the hands of the American people.

GEORGE WASHINGTON (U.S. president, 1732–1799)
First Inaugural Address, April 30, 1789

the **basics**

Freedom is a very dangerous thing. Anything else is disastrous.

JAMES BALDWIN (U.S. writer, 1924–1987)

Freedom, *n.* A political condition that every nation supposes itself to enjoy in virtual monopoly.

AMBROSE BIERCE (U.S. journalist, 1842–1915)

The difference between liberty and liberties is as great as between God and gods.

LUDWIG BOERNE (German journalist, 1786–1837)

Freedom—it is today more than ever the most precious human possession.

PEARL BUCK (U.S. writer, 1892–1973),
Nobel Prize (in literature) acceptance address,
Stockholm, Sweden, December 1938

Any great love involves sacrifice. You feel that as a father, as a husband. You give up all your freedom. But the love is so much greater than the freedom.

NICHOLAS CAGE (contemporary U.S. actor)

Freedom is participation in power.

CICERO (Roman statesman, first century B.C.)

Liberty, like charity, must begin at home.

JAMES B. CONANT (U.S. educator, 1893–1978)

Liberty is the capacity to do anything that does no harm to others.

DECLARATION OF THE RIGHTS OF MAN AND THE CITIZEN, France, Article 4, 1789

Freedom is the right to be wrong, not the right to do wrong.

JOHN G. DIEFENBAKER (Canadian
prime minister, 1895–1975)

We are made of contradictions—our freedom is necessary.

RALPH WALDO EMERSON (U.S. philosopher, 1803–1882)

The most vital right is the right to love and be loved.

EMMA GOLDMAN (Lithuanian-born U.S.
political activist and writer, 1869–1940)

Natural liberty is a gift of the beneficent Creator to the whole human race.

ALEXANDER HAMILTON (West Indian-born
U.S. secretary of the treasury, 1755–1804)

The spirit of liberty is the spirit which is not too sure that it is right; the spirit of liberty is the spirit which seeks to understand the minds of other men and women; the spirit of liberty is the spirit which weighs their interests alongside its own without bias.

LEARNED HAND (U.S. jurist, 1872–1961)

The price of freedom of religion or of speech or of the press is that we must put up with . . . a good deal of rubbish.

ROBERT H. JACKSON (U.S. Supreme Court associate justice, 1892–1954)

Without freedom there can be no morality.

CARL G. JUNG (Swiss psychiatrist, 1875–1961)

The most important tenet of Tibetan Buddhist teaching is compassion, but to try to practice this, one must be free.

KARMAPA (contemporary Tibetan Buddhist monk)

The political problem of mankind is to combine three things: **ECONOMIC EFFICIENCY, SOCIAL JUSTICE, AND INDIVIDUAL LIBERTY.**

JOHN MAYNARD KEYNES (English economist, 1883–1946)

Freedom's just another word for nothin' left to lose.

KRIS KRISTOFFERSON and FRED FOSTER (contemporary U.S. songwriters), "Me and Bobby McGee"

If I have freedom in my love,
And in my soul am free,
Angels alone that soar above
Enjoy such liberty.

RICHARD LOVELACE (English poet, 1618–1657),
"To Althea, from Prison"

I believe in only one thing: liberty; but I do not believe in liberty enough to want to force it upon anyone.

H. L. MENCKEN (U.S. journalist, 1880–1956)

Until you lose your reputation, you never realize what a burden it was or what freedom really is.

MARGARET MITCHELL (U.S. writer, 1900–1949)

Freedom of speech, freedom of the press, and freedom of religion all have a double aspect—freedom of thought and freedom of action.

FRANK MURPHY (Michigan governor and U.S. Supreme Court associate justice, 1890–1959)

No arsenal or no weapon in the arsenals of the world is so formidable as the will and moral courage of free men and women.

RONALD REAGAN (contemporary U.S. president), *First Inaugural Address,* January 20,1981

Freedom breeds freedom. Nothing else does.

ANNE ROE (contemporary U.S. psychologist and educator)

Oh liberty, oh liberty, what crimes are committed in thy name!

> MARIE-JEANNE ROLAND (French revolutionary figure,1754–1793), last words before being guillotined, November 8, 1793

To renounce liberty is to renounce being a man.

> JEAN-JACQUES ROUSSEAU (French philosopher, 1712–1778)

Freedom is what you do with what's been done to you.

> JEAN-PAUL SARTRE (French philosopher, 1905–1980)

Human beings are highly predictable as physiochemical systems; less so as living bodies; much less so as conscious beings; and hardly at all as self-aware persons. The reason for this unpredictability [lies] . . . in the nature of freedom.

> E. F. SCHUMACHER (German-born British economist, 1911–1977)

Freedom near at hand makes an old man brave.

SENECA the YOUNGER (Roman philosopher and
statesman, first century A.D.)

**My definition of a free society is a society where it is
safe to be unpopular.**

We have confused the free with the free and easy.

ADLAI E. STEVENSON (Illinois governor, presidential
candidate, and UN ambassador, 1900–1965)

Future generations will yet win many a liberty of which
we do not even feel the want.

MAX STIRNER (German philosopher, 1806–1856)

Afoot and light-hearted I take to the open road,
Healthy, free, the world before me,
The long brown path before leading wherever I choose.

WALT WHITMAN (U.S. poet, 1819–1892),
"Song of the Open Road"

Sometimes naked, sometimes mad; now as a sage,
now as a fool; thus they appear on earth, the free ones.

ANONYMOUS (HINDU)

Freedom Is Not Free.

ANONYMOUS (U.S.), inscription on the Korean War
Memorial, Washington, D.C., dedicated in July 1995

Above all, liberty.

SAYING (GREEK)

The right to wave your fist ends where your neighbor's
nose begins.

SAYING (U.S.)

CONSCIENCE
conscience

We should begin by setting conscience free.

JOHN ADAMS (U.S. president, 1735–1826)

I will stay in jail to the end of my days before I make a butchery of my conscience.

JOHN BUNYAN (English preacher and writer, 1628–1688)

Whilst . . . [conscience] is a good guide for individual conduct, imposition of that conduct upon all will be an insufferable interference with everybody's freedom of conscience.

MOHANDAS K. GANDHI (Indian spiritual
and nationalist leader, 1869–1948)

FREEDOM OF CONSCIENCE IS A NATURAL RIGHT, both antecedent and superior to all human laws and institutions whatever: a right which laws never gave and which laws [can] never take away.

JOHN GOODWIN (English writer, 1594–1665)

Any attempt to replace the personal conscience by a collective conscience does violence to the individual and is the first step toward totalitarianism.

HERMANN HESSE (German writer, 1877–1962)

We are bound, you, I, and everyone, to make common cause, even with error itself, to maintain the common right of freedom of conscience.

THOMAS JEFFERSON (U.S. president, 1743–1826)

The one thing that doesn't abide by majority rule is a person's conscience.

HARPER LEE (contemporary U.S. writer)

I cannot and will not recant anything, for to go against conscience is neither right nor safe. Here I stand. I cannot do no other, so help me God. Amen.

MARTIN LUTHER (German religious reformer, 1483–1546)

I have the right to believe freely, to be a slave to no man's authority. If this be heresy, so be it. It is still the truth. To go against conscience is neither right nor safe. I will not recant. **NO MAN CAN COMMAND MY CONSCIENCE.**

BEN SHAHN (Lithuanian-born U.S. artist, 1898–1969)

Must the citizen ever for a moment, or in the least degree, resign his conscience to the legislator? Why has every man a conscience then? I think that we should be men first, and subjects afterwards. It is not desirable to cultivate a respect for the law, so much as for the right. The only obligation which I have a right to assume is to do at any time what I think right.

HENRY DAVID THOREAU (U.S. philosopher, 1817–1862), "Civil Disobedience" (essay)

While we are contending for our own liberty, we should be very cautious of violating the rights of conscience in others, ever considering that God alone is the Judge of the Hearts of Men, and to him only in this Case, they are answerable.

GEORGE WASHINGTON (U.S. president, 1732–1799)

creativity

What that energy, which is the life of genius, above everything demands and insists upon is freedom; entire independence of all authority, prescription and routine- the fullest room to expand as it will.

MATTHEW ARNOLD (English poet and critic, 1822–1888)

Without freedom, no art; art lives only on the restraints it imposes on itself, and dies of all others.

There is not a single true work of art that has not in the end added to the inner freedom of each person who has known and loved it.

ALBERT CAMUS (French writer, 1913–1960)

I have steadily endeavored to keep my mind free so as to give up any hypothesis, however much beloved [and I cannot resist forming one on every subject], as soon as facts are shown to be opposed to it.

CHARLES DARWIN (English naturalist, 1809–1882)

M. A. ROSANOFF: Mr. Edison, please tell me what laboratory rules you want me to observe.

EDISON: Hell! there *ain't* no rules around here! We're trying to accomplish somep'n!

THOMAS ALVA EDISON (U.S. inventor, 1847–1931)

One can organize to apply a discovery already made, but not to make one. **ONLY A FREE INDIVIDUAL CAN MAKE A DISCOVERY. . . .** Can you imagine an organization of scientists making the discoveries of Charles Darwin?

ALBERT EINSTEIN (German-born
U.S. physicist, 1879–1955)

What has been best done in the world—the works of genius—cost nothing. There is no painful effort, but it is the spontaneous flowing of the thought. Shakespeare made his Hamlet as a bird weaves its nest.

RALPH WALDO EMERSON (U.S.
philosopher, 1803–1882)

It isn't like a big thing of, you know, you gotta take a thunderbolt and throw it at Zeus, except every once in a while, but that comes on its own. Zeusie and thunderbolts come on their own; you can't call them up. They're products of circumstance, and time, and history, and yourself, and your metabolism, and your love affairs, and your money, and your lack of money, and your food, and your drugs, and your shoes, and your Brooks Brothers, and your Empire State Building, and the winter snow, and your mother's living death, or something. So you can't combine all those things on your own. You have to wait for nature to throw up a great wave.

ALLEN GINSBERG (U.S. poet, 1926–1997)

You can produce plenty of goods without much freedom, but the whole creative life of man is ultimately impossible without a considerable measure of individual freedom, of initiative.

ALDOUS HUXLEY (English writer, 1894–1963)

Creativity and innovation always build on the past; the past always tries to control the creativity that builds upon it; **FREE SOCIETIES ENABLE THE FUTURE BY LIMIT-ING THIS POWER OF THE PAST; OURS IS LESS AND LESS A FREE SOCIETY.**

LAWRENCE LESSIG (contemporary U.S. professor of law)

The artist produces for the liberation of his soul. It is his nature to create as it is the nature of water to run down hill.

W. SOMERSET MAUGHAM (English writer, 1874–1965)

Encounters taking the form of challenge-and-response are the most illuminating kind of events for a student of human affairs if he believes, as I believe, that one of the most distinctive characteristics of Man is that he is partially free to make choices. . . . Encounters are the occasions in human life on which freedom and creativity come into play and on which new things are brought into existence.

ARNOLD J. TOYNBEE (English historian, 1889–1975)

DEMOCRACY
democracy

**NO RIGHT IS MORE PRECIOUS IN A FREE
COUNTRY THAN THAT OF HAVING A VOICE
IN THE ELECTION OF THOSE WHO MAKE
THE LAWS** . . . [because] other rights, even the most
basic, are illusory if the right to vote is undermined.

HUGO L. BLACK (U.S. Supreme Court
associate justice, 1886–1971)

Without an unfettered press, without liberty of speech,
all the outward forms and structures of free institutions
are a sham, a pretense—the sheerest mockery. If the
press is not free; if speech is not independent and
untrammeled; if the mind is shackled or made impotent
through fear, it makes no difference under what form of
government you live you are a subject and not a citizen.
Republics are not in and of themselves better than other
forms of government except in so far as they carry with
them and guarantee to the citizen that liberty of thought
and action for which they were established.

WILLIAM E. BORAH (Idaho senator, 1865–1940)

A system of democracy implies a government in which
ultimate political authority is vested in the people. The

aspirations of a democracy are lofty; they celebrate the individual, personal liberty, equal political rights, and they are based on the noble premise that **THE PEOPLE CAN BE THE MASTERS OF THEIR OWN DESTINY.**

THOMAS E. CRONIN (contemporary U.S. political scientist)

The major achievement of the Free Society is in the ability to change the status quo without violence, to cast a current practice into limbo and adopt a new one by an election, to remake the economy or renovate an institution, yet not destroy it, to refashion even the structure of government by votes rather than by force.

WILLIAM O. DOUGLAS (U.S. Supreme Court associate justice, 1898–1980)

Human dignity, economic freedom, individual responsibility, these are the characteristics that distinguish democracy from all other forms [of government].

DWIGHT D. EISENHOWER (U.S. president, 1890–1969)

The very purpose of a Bill of Rights was to withdraw certain subjects from the vicissitudes of political controversy, to place them beyond the reach of majorities and officials and to establish them as legal principles to be applied by the courts. **ONE'S RIGHT TO LIFE, LIBERTY, AND PROPERTY, TO FREE SPEECH, A FREE PRESS, FREEDOM OF WORSHIP AND ASSEMBLY, AND OTHER FUNDAMENTAL RIGHTS MAY NOT BE SUBMITTED TO VOTE; THEY DEPEND ON THE OUTCOME OF NO ELECTIONS.**

ROBERT H. JACKSON (U.S. Supreme Court associate justice, 1892–1954)

No man is good enough to govern another man, without that other's consent. I say this is the leading principle—the sheet anchor—of American republicanism.

As I would not be a slave, so I would not be a master. This expresses my idea of democracy. Whatever differs from this, to the extent of the difference, is no democracy.

ABRAHAM LINCOLN (U.S. president, 1809–1865)

The three elements of democratic activity—timely information, the technology to communicate with one another, and then mobilization for action and results.

RALPH NADER (contemporary U.S. consumer advocate and presidential candidate)

Our constitution does not copy the laws of neighboring states; we are rather a pattern to others than imitators ourselves. Its administration favors the many instead of the few; this is why it is called a democracy. If we look to the laws, they afford equal justice to all in their private differences; if to social standing, advancement in public life falls to reputation for capacity, class considerations not being allowed to interfere with merit; nor again does poverty bar the way; if a man is able to serve the state, he is not hindered by the obscurity of his condition. The freedom which we enjoy in our government extends also to our ordinary life.

PERICLES (Greek statesman, fifth century B.C.), Funeral Oration, 431 B.C.

Freedom . . . in a democracy is the glory of the state.

PLATO (Greek philosopher, fourth century B.C.), *The Republic*

No democracy can long survive which does not accept as fundamental to its very existence the recognition of the rights of minorities.

FRANKLIN D. ROOSEVELT (U.S. president, 1882–1945)

Self-government, if it means anything, means the exercise of sufficient self-restraint on the part of the people to uphold their own fundamental law against every temptation to subvert it. In the last analysis, the continued existence of the republic itself depends upon the faithful maintenance of that course, and can survive no other, for only thus can we preserve the character of our institutions as a government of laws and prevent their degeneration into a chaos of fleeting and fickle emotion.

GEORGE SUTHERLAND (U.S. Supreme Court associate justice, 1862–1942)

The foundation of democracy is the sense of spiritual independence which nerves the individual to stand alone against the powers of this world.

R. H. TAWNEY (English economic historian, 1880–1962)

Democracy extends the sphere of individual freedom; socialism restricts it. Democracy attaches all possible value to each man; socialism makes each man a mere agent, a mere number. Democracy and socialism have nothing in common but one word: equality. But notice the difference: while democracy seeks equality in liberty, socialism seeks equality in restraint and servitude.

ALEXIS de TOCQUEVILLE (French statesman and writer, 1805–1859)

The world must be made safe for democracy. Its peace must be planted upon the tested foundations of political liberty.

WOODROW WILSON (U.S. president, 1856–1924)

economics

If we are serious about reducing the size of government and its burdens, then we need to return economic self-determination to the people. And we must not do this by inviting in destructive industries to "provide jobs"; we must do it by fostering economic democracy. **WE MUST DO EVERYTHING POSSIBLE TO ASSURE ORDINARY CITIZENS THE POSSIBILITY OF OWNING A SMALL, USABLE SHARE OF THE COUNTRY.**

WENDELL BERRY (contemporary U.S. farmer and writer)

We can have democracy in this country or we can have great wealth concentrated in the hands of a few, but we can't have both.

LOUIS D. BRANDEIS (U.S. Supreme Court associate justice, 1856–1941)

Money is coined liberty.

FYODOR DOSTOYEVSKY (Russian writer, 1821–1881)

Property has its duties as well as its rights.

THOMAS DRUMMOND (British engineer, 1797–1840)

Think what you do when you run in debt; you give to another power over your liberty.

BENJAMIN FRANKLIN (U.S. printer, inventor, and statesman, 1706–1790)

Economic freedom is a necessary but not sufficient condition for political freedom. . . . Political freedom in turn is a necessary condition for the long-term maintenance of economic freedom.

MILTON FRIEDMAN (contemporary U.S. economist)

The general evidence of repression poses an ancient contradiction for capitalism: while [capitalism] claims to promote human freedom, it profits concretely from the denial of freedom, most especially freedom for the workers employed by capitalist enterprise.

WILLIAM GREIDER (contemporary U.S. writer)

Liberty is a word that rumbles meaninglessly in empty bellies.

MARK HATFIELD (contemporary Oregon senator)

Free competition is worth more to society than it costs.

OLIVER WENDELL HOLMES JR. (U.S. Supreme Court chief justice, 1841–1935)

I am one of those who do not believe that a national debt is a national blessing, but rather a curse to a republic; inasmuch as it is calculated to raise around the administration a moneyed aristocracy dangerous to the liberties of the country.

ANDREW JACKSON (U.S. president, 1767–1845)

LIVES BASED ON HAVING ARE LESS FREE THAN LIVES BASED EITHER ON DOING OR ON BEING.

WILLIAM JAMES (U.S. physician, psychologist, and philosopher, 1842–1910)

Agriculture, manufactures, commerce, and navigation, the four pillars of our prosperity, are the most thriving when left to individual enterprise.

THOMAS JEFFERSON (U.S. president, 1743–1826)

If a free society cannot help the many who are poor, it cannot save the few who are rich.

JOHN F. KENNEDY (U.S. president, 1917–1963),
Inaugural Address, January 20, 1961

Separate property from private possession, and liberty is erased.

RUSSELL KIRK (U.S. writer, 1918–1994)

Property is the fruit of labor—is a positive good in the world. That some should be rich, shows that others may become rich, and hence is just encouragement to industry and enterprise. Let not him who is homeless pull down the house of another, but let him work diligently and build one for himself, thus by example assuring that his own shall be safe from violence when built.

ABRAHAM LINCOLN (U.S. president, 1809–1865)

The free market should not include the right to pollute our environment.

GEORGE S. McGOVERN (contemporary South Dakota senator and presidential candidate)

There are only two kinds of freedom in the world: the freedom of the rich and powerful, and the freedom of the artist and the monk who renounce possessions.

ANAÏS NIN (French-born U.S. writer, 1903–1977)

GIVE ME AGAIN MY HOLLOW TREE
A CRUST OF BREAD, AND LIBERTY!

ALEXANDER POPE (English poet, 1688–1744),
Imitations of Horace

A democracy cannot flourish half rich and half poor, any more than it can flourish half free and half slave.

FELIX G. ROHATYN (contemporary Austrian-born
U.S. financier and ambassador)

True individual freedom cannot exist without economic security and independence. **PEOPLE WHO ARE HUNGRY AND OUT OF A JOB ARE THE STUFF OF WHICH DICTATORSHIPS ARE MADE.**

FRANKLIN D. ROOSEVELT (U.S. president, 1882–1945)

In every civilized society property rights must be carefully safeguarded; ordinarily and in the great majority of cases, human rights and property rights are fundamentally and in the long run, identical; but when it clearly appears that there is a real conflict between them, human rights must have the upper hand; for property belongs to man and not man to property.

THEODORE ROOSEVELT (U.S. president, 1858–1919)

Advocates of capitalism are very apt to appeal to the sacred principles of liberty, which are all embodied in one maxim: The fortunate must not be restrained in the exercise of tyranny over the unfortunate.

BERTRAND RUSSELL (English mathematician and philosopher, 1872–1970)

[Under the system of natural liberty,] every man, as long as he does not violate the laws of justice, is left perfectly free to pursue his own interest his own way and to bring both his industry and capital into competition with those of any other man or order of men.

ADAM SMITH (Scottish economist and philosopher, 1723–1790), *The Wealth of Nations*

Freedom is not an ideal, it is not even a protection, if it means nothing more than freedom to stagnate, to live without dreams, to have no greater aim than a second car and another television set.

ADLAI E. STEVENSON (Illinois governor, presidential candidate, and UN ambassador, 1900–1965)

The price we have to pay for money is paid in liberty.

ROBERT LOUIS STEVENSON (Scottish writer, 1850–1894)

Commerce renders men independent of one another, gives them a lofty notion of their personal importance, leads them to seek to conduct their own affairs, and teaches how to conduct them well; it therefore prepares men for freedom, but preserves them from revolutions.

Those who prize freedom only for the material benefits it offers have never kept it for long.

ALEXIS de TOCQUEVILLE (French statesman and writer, 1805–1859), *Democracy in America*

CHAINS OF GOLD, STILL A SLAVE.

SAYING (ENGLISH)

Everyone has the right to a standard of living adequate for the health and well-being of himself and of his family, including food, clothing, housing and medical care and necessary social services, and the right to security in the event of unemployment, sickness, disability, widowhood, old age or other lack of livelihood in circumstances beyond his control.

UNIVERSAL DECLARATION OF HUMAN RIGHTS,
United Nations, Article 25.1, 1948

EDUCATION
education

THE SECRET OF EDUCATION LIES IN RESPECTING THE PUPIL. It is not for you to choose what he shall know, what he shall do. It is chosen and foreordained, and he only holds the key to his own secret. . . . Respect the child. Wait and see the new product of nature. Nature loves analogies, but not repetitions. Respect the child. Be not too much his parent. Trespass not on his solitude.

RALPH WALDO EMERSON (U.S. philosopher, 1803–1882)

I know no safe depository of the ultimate powers of the society but the people themselves; and if we think them not enlightened enough to exercise their control with a wholesome discretion, the remedy is not to take it from them, but to inform their discretion by education.

THOMAS JEFFERSON (U.S. president, 1743–1826)

Have you ever been at sea in a dense fog, when it seemed as if a tangible white darkness shut you in and the great ship, tense and anxious, groped her way toward the shore with plummet and sounding-line, and you waited with beating heart for something to happen?

I was like that ship before my education began, only I was without compass or sounding line, and no way of knowing how near the harbor was. **"LIGHT! GIVE ME LIGHT!"** was the wordless cry of my soul, and the light of love shone on me in that very hour.

HELEN KELLER (U.S. writer and lecturer, 1880–1968). Keller lost her sight and hearing when she was nineteen months old.

Education aims at independence of judgment. Propaganda offers ready-made opinions for the unthinking herd. Education and propaganda are directly opposed both in aim and method.

EVERETT DEAN MARTIN (U.S. psychologist, 1880–1941)

It is easy to substitute our will for that of the child by means of suggestion or coercion; but when we have done this we have robbed him of his greatest right, the right to construct his own personality.

MARIA MONTESSORI (Italian physician and educator, 1870–1952)

These teachers of submission! Wherever there is anything small and sick and scabby, there they crawl like
lice; and only my disgust stops me from cracking them.

FRIEDRICH NIETZSCHE (German philosopher, 1844–1900)

Education should have two objects: first, to give definite knowledge, reading and writing, language and
mathematics, and so on; secondly, to create those
mental habits which will enable people to acquire
knowledge and form sound judgments for themselves.

BERTRAND RUSSELL (English mathematician and
philosopher, 1872–1970)

As the base rhetorician uses language to increase his
own power, to produce converts to his own cause, and
to create loyal followers of his own person—so the
noble rhetorician uses language to wean men away
from their inclination to depend on authority, to encour-
age them to think and speak clearly, and to teach them
to be their own masters.

THOMAS S. SZASZ (contemporary
Hungarian-born U.S. psychiatrist)

Education is effective in proportion to the degree of its voluntariness.

ARNOLD J. TOYNBEE (English historian, 1889–1975)

The only avenue towards wisdom is by freedom in the presence of knowledge. But the only avenue towards knowledge is by discipline in the acquirement of ordered fact. . . .

The two principles, **FREEDOM AND DISCIPLINE, ARE NOT ANTAGONISTS,** but should be so adjusted in the child's life that they correspond to a natural sway, to and fro, of the developing personality.

It is necessary in life to have acquired the habit of cheerfully undertaking imposed tasks. The conditions can be satisfied if the tasks correspond to the natural cravings of the pupil at his stage of progress, if they keep his powers at full stretch, if they attain an obviously sensible result, and if reasonable freedom is allowed in the mode of execution.

ALFRED NORTH WHITEHEAD (English
mathematician and philosopher, 1861–1947)

The most perfect education . . . is such an exercise of the understanding as is best calculated to strengthen the body and form the heart. Or, in other words, to enable the individual to attain such habits of virtue as will render it independent.

MARY WOLLSTONECRAFT (English writer, 1759–1797)

equality

The real democratic American idea is, not that every man shall be on a level with every other man, but that every man shall have liberty to be what God made him without hindrance.

HENRY WARD BEECHER (U.S. clergyman, 1813–1887)

In respect of their rights men are born and remain free and equal.

DECLARATION OF THE RIGHTS OF MAN
AND THE CITIZEN, France, Article 1, 1789

A society that puts equality—in the sense of equality of outcome—ahead of freedom will end up with neither equality nor freedom. **THE USE OF FORCE TO ACHIEVE EQUALITY WILL DESTROY FREEDOM, AND THE FORCE, INTRODUCED FOR GOOD PURPOSES, WILL END UP IN THE HANDS OF PEOPLE WHO USE IT TO PROMOTE THEIR OWN INTERESTS.**

MILTON FRIEDMAN and ROSE FRIEDMAN
(contemporary U.S. economists)

Nobody's free until everybody's free.

FANNIE LOU HAMER (U.S. human
rights leader, 1917–1977)

EQUALITY OF OPPORTUNITY IS THE RIGHT OF EVERY AMERICAN—RICH OR POOR, FOREIGN OR NATIVE-BORN, IRRESPECTIVE OF FAITH OR COLOR. . . . Only from confidence that this right will be upheld can flow that unbounded courage and hope which stimulate each individual man and woman to endeavor and to achievement. The sum of their achievement is the gigantic harvest of national progress.

HERBERT HOOVER (U.S. president, 1874–1964)

Rightful liberty is unobstructed action according to our will within limits drawn around us by the equal rights of others.

THOMAS JEFFERSON (U.S. president, 1743–1826)

Is true Freedom but to break
Fetters for our own dear sake,
And, with leathern hearts, forget
That we owe mankind a debt?
No! True Freedom is to share
All the chains our brothers wear,
And, with heart and hand, to be
Earnest to make others free!

JAMES RUSSELL LOWELL (U.S. poet, 1819–1891),
"Stanzas on Freedom"

YOUR FREEDOM AND MINE CANNOT BE SEPARATED.

NELSON MANDELA (contemporary South African
president and human rights leader)

All we got to say on the proposition that all men are created equal is this: first, you and me is as good as anybody else, and maybe a damn sight better.

H. L. MENCKEN (U.S. journalist, 1880–1956)

I am angry that so many of the sons of the powerful and well-placed and so many professional athletes (who were probably healthier than any of us) managed to wangle slots in Reserve and National Guard units. Of the many tragedies of Vietnam, this raw class discrimination strikes me as the most damaging to the ideal that all Americans are created equal and owe equal allegiance to their country.

COLIN L. POWELL (contemporary U.S. secretary of state), 1995

Who ever walked behind anyone to freedom? If we can't go hand in hand, I don't want to go.

HAZEL SCOTT (Trinidad-born U.S. singer and actor, 1920–1981)

Recognition of the inherent dignity and of the equal and inalienable rights of all members of the human family is the foundation of freedom, justice and peace in the world.

UNIVERSAL DECLARATION OF HUMAN RIGHTS, United Nations, Preamble, 1948

The opportunity of an education . . . is a right which must be made available to all on equal terms. . . .

In the field of public education the doctrine of "separate but equal" has no place. Separate educational facilities are inherently unequal.

EARL WARREN (U.S. Supreme Court chief justice, 1891–1974), *Brown v. Board of Education of Topeka,* Kansas, 1954

❧ ❧

Liberty, Equality, Fraternity.
[Liberté, Egalité, Fraternité.]

SLOGAN, French Revolution, 1789

free **WILL AND DESTINY**

Everywhere the human soul stands between a hemisphere of light and another of darkness; on the confines of two everlasting hostile empires, Necessity and Free Will.

THOMAS CARLYLE (English historian, 1795–1881)

The glory of human nature lies in our seeming capacity to exercise conscious control of our own destiny.

WINSTON CHURCHILL (British prime minister, 1874–1965)

I think that the human race does command its own destiny and that that destiny can eventually embrace the stars.

LORRAINE HANSBERRY (U.S. writer, 1930–1965)

History is often cruel, and rarely logical, and yet the wisest of realists are those who recognize that fate can indeed be shaped by human faith and courage.

HENRY A. KISSINGER (contemporary
German-born U.S. secretary of state)

God will not do everything, in order not to deprive us of free will and the portion of the glory that falls to our lot.

NICCOLÒ MACHIAVELLI (Italian political
philosopher, 1469–1527), *The Prince*

Brave men earn the right to shape their own destiny.

ARTHUR M. SCHLESINGER JR.
(contemporary U.S. historian)

Men at some time are masters of their fates:
The fault, dear Brutus, is not in our stars,
But in ourselves, that we are underlings.

WILLIAM SHAKESPEARE (English
playwright, 1564–1616), *Julius Caesar*

We must believe in free will. We have no choice.

ISAAC BASHEVIS SINGER (Polish-born
U.S. writer, 1904–1991)

History does not make history. Men and women make foreign policy decisions. . . . Often, after a war or other national calamity, historians look back and speak of fate or inevitability. But such historical determinism merely becomes a metaphor for the evasion of responsibility. There is, after all, in our lives, a measure of free will and self-determination.

JOHN G. STOESSINGER (contemporary
Austrian-born U.S. political scientist)

WE ARE THE CHOICES WE HAVE MADE.

MERYL STREEP (contemporary U.S. actor)

Every human being is the artificer of his own fate. . . . Events, circumstances, etc., have their origin in ourselves. They spring from seeds which we have sown.

HENRY DAVID THOREAU (U.S. philosopher, 1817–1862)

Around every man a fatal circle is traced beyond which he cannot pass; but within the wide verge of that circle he is powerful and free; as it is with man, so with communities.

ALEXIS de TOCQUEVILLE (French statesman and writer, 1805–1859)

A human being may be defined as a personality with a will of its own capable of making moral choices between good and evil.

ARNOLD J. TOYNBEE (English historian, 1889–1975)

Liberty. . . consists in the ability to choose.

SIMONE WEIL (French writer, 1909–1943)

Acting as if we are free is a way of resolving the paradox of determinism and freedom.

HOWARD ZINN (contemporary U.S. historian)

Free will and determinism are like a game of cards. The hand that is dealt you represents determinism. The way you play your hand represents free will.

ANONYMOUS (INDIAN)

freedom
defended

FREEDOM COMES AT A PRICE—and tragically, sometimes that price is the commitment to defend freedom by arms. No matter how painful, America understands its obligations to its citizens, and the citizens of the world. America has been, is and always will be willing to do its duty—to sacrifice even its own blood so that people everywhere can live as individuals, responsible for their own destinies.

MICHAEL R. BLOOMBERG
(contemporary New York City mayor),
United Nations address, September 13, 2002

The great struggles of the 20th century between liberty and totalitarianism ended with a decisive victory for the forces of freedom and a single sustainable model for national success: freedom, democracy and free enterprise. In the 21st century, only nations that share a commitment to protecting basic human rights and guaranteeing political and economic freedom will

be able to unleash the potential of their people and assure their future prosperity. People everywhere want to say what they think, choose who will govern them, worship as they please, educate their children (male and female), own property and enjoy the benefits of their labor. These values of freedom are right and true for every person, in every society—and the duty of protecting these values against their enemies is the common calling of freedom-loving people across the globe.

GEORGE W. BUSH (contemporary U.S. president), The National Security Strategy of the United States, September 19, 2002

We shall defend our island, whatever the cost may be. We shall fight on the beaches, we shall fight on the landing grounds, we shall fight in the fields and in the streets, we shall fight in the hills; we shall never surrender.

WINSTON CHURCHILL (British prime minister, 1874–1965), House of Commons speech, June 4,1940, Britain's darkest moment during World War II (following the evacuation at Dunkirk)

I would remind you that extremism in the defense of liberty is no vice. And let me remind you also that moderation in the pursuit of justice is no virtue.

BARRY M. GOLDWATER (Arizona senator
and presidential candidate, 1909–1998)

Freedom is fragile and must be protected. To sacrifice it, even as a temporary measure, is to betray it.

GERMAINE GREER (contemporary Australian writer)

The Supreme Court has always been the last bastion of the protection of our freedoms.

BARBARA JORDAN (Texas congresswoman, 1936–1996)

Let every nation know, whether it wishes us well or ill, that we shall pay any price, bear any burden, meet any hardship, support any friend, oppose any foe to assure the survival and the success of liberty.

JOHN F. KENNEDY (U.S. president, 1917–1963),
Inaugural Address, January 20, 1961

Precisely because the Lager [i.e., camp] was a great machine to reduce us to beasts, we must not become beasts; that even in this place one can survive, and therefore one must want to survive, to tell the story, to bear witness; and that to survive we must force ourselves to save at least the skeleton, the scaffolding, the form of civilization. We are slaves, deprived of every right, exposed to every insult, condemned to certain death, but **WE STILL POSSESS ONE POWER, AND WE MUST DEFEND IT WITH ALL OUR STRENGTH FOR IT IS THE LAST—THE POWER TO REFUSE OUR CONSENT.**

> PRIMO LEVI (Italian chemist, writer, and Auschwitz survivor, 1919–1987)

They have rights who dare maintain them.

> JAMES RUSSELL LOWELL (U.S. poet, 1819–1891)

The rights and interests of every or any person are only secure from being disregarded when the person interested is himself able and habitually disposed to stand up for them.

> JOHN STUART MILL (English philosopher, 1806–1873)

He that would make his own liberty secure must guard even his enemy from oppression; for if he violates this duty he establishes a precedent that will reach to himself.

THOMAS PAINE (English-born U.S. political philosopher, 1737–1809)

ETERNAL VIGILANCE IS THE PRICE OF LIBERTY.

WENDELL PHILLIPS (U.S. abolitionist and social reformer, 1811–1884)

My belief has always been . . . that wherever in this land any individual's constitutional rights are being unjustly denied, it is the obligation of the federal government—at point of bayonet if necessary—to restore that individual's constitutional rights.

RONALD REAGAN (contemporary U.S. president)

It is not the fact of liberty but the way in which liberty is exercised that ultimately determines whether liberty itself survives.

DOROTHY THOMPSON (U.S. journalist, 1894–1961)

Irreverence is the champion of liberty and its only sure defense.

MARK TWAIN (U.S. writer and humorist, 1835–1910)

The true character of liberty is independence, maintained by force.

VOLTAIRE (French philosopher, 1694–1778)

freedom
endangered

Experience should teach us to be most on our guard to protect liberty when the government's purposes are beneficent. Men born to freedom are naturally alert to repel invasion of their liberty by evil-minded rulers. **THE GREATEST DANGERS TO LIBERTY LURK IN INSIDIOUS ENCROACHMENT BY MEN OF ZEAL, WELL-MEANING BUT WITHOUT UNDERSTANDING.**

LOUIS D. BRANDEIS (U.S. Supreme Court associate justice, 1856–1941)

Those who would give up essential liberty to purchase a little temporary safety deserve neither liberty nor safety.

BENJAMIN FRANKLIN (U.S. printer, inventor, and statesman, 1706–1790)

The great threat to freedom is the concentration of power.

MILTON FRIEDMAN (contemporary U.S. economist)

The power of concentrated finance, the power of self-ish pressure groups, the power of any class organized in opposition to the whole—any one of these, when allowed to dominate, is fully capable of destroying individual freedom as is power concentrated in the political head of the state.

In the councils of government, we must guard against the acquisition of unwarranted influence, whether sought or unsought, by the military-industrial complex. The potential for the disastrous rise of misplaced power exists and will persist. We must never let the weight of this combination endanger our liberties or democratic processes. We should take nothing for granted.

DWIGHT D. EISENHOWER
(U.S. president, 1890–1969)

IF MEN AND WOMEN ARE IN CHAINS ANYWHERE IN THE WORLD, THEN FREEDOM IS ENDANGERED EVERYWHERE.

JOHN F. KENNEDY (U.S. president, 1917–1963)

Our reliance is in the love of liberty which God has planted in our bosoms. Our defense is in the preservation of the spirit which prizes liberty as the heritage of all men, in all lands, everywhere. Destroy this spirit, and you have planted the seeds of despotism around your own doors. Familiarize yourselves with the chains of bondage, and you are preparing your own limbs to wear them. Accustomed to trample on the rights of those around you, you have lost the genius of your own independence, and become the fit subjects of the first cunning tyrant who rises [among you].

ABRAHAM LINCOLN (U.S. president, 1809–1865)

There are more instances of the abridgment of the freedom of the people by gradual and silent encroachments of those in power than by violent and sudden usurpations.

JAMES MADISON (U.S. president, 1751–1836)

Today the large organization is lord and master, and most of its employees have been desensitized much as were the medieval peasants who never knew they were serfs.

RALPH NADER (contemporary U.S. consumer advocate and presidential candidate)

THE LIBERTY OF A DEMOCRACY IS NOT SAFE IF THE PEOPLE TOLERATE THE GROWTH OF PRIVATE POWER TO A POINT WHERE IT BECOMES STRONGER THAN THEIR DEMOCRATIC STATE ITSELF. THAT, IN ITS ESSENCE, IS FASCISM—OWNERSHIP OF GOVERNMENT BY AN INDIVIDUAL, BY A GROUP, OR BY ANY OTHER CONTROLLING PRIVATE POWER.

FRANKLIN D. ROOSEVELT (U.S. president, 1882–1945)

The untrammeled intensification of laissez-faire capitalism and the spread of market values into all areas of life is endangering our open and democratic society.

GEORGE SOROS (contemporary Hungarian-born U.S. financier)

Rulers who destroy men's freedom commonly begin by trying to retain its forms. . . . They cherish the illusion that they can combine the prerogatives of absolute power with the moral authority that comes from popular assent.

ALEXIS de TOCQUEVILLE (French statesman and writer, 1805–1859)

They will avoid the necessity of those overgrown military establishments which, under any form of government, are inauspicious to liberty, and which are to be regarded as particularly hostile to republican liberty.

GEORGE WASHINGTON (U.S. president, 1732–1799), *Farewell Address,* September 17, 1796

FREEDOM
lost

It is a strange desire to seek power and to lose liberty, or to seek power over others and to lose power over [one's] self.

> FRANCIS BACON (English philosopher, 1561–1616)

Our liberty cannot be taken away unless the people are themselves accomplices.

> LORD BOLINGBROKE (English
> political leader, 1678–1751)

The people never give up their liberties but under some delusion.

> EDMUND BURKE (British statesman
> and philosopher, 1729–1797)

A system of mal-government begins by refusing man his rights, and ends by depriving him of the power of appreciating the value of that which he has lost.

> C. C. COLTON (English clergyman and writer, 1780–1832)

Political and economic liberty decays for the same reason . . . that moral laxity increases: because the family and the church have ceased to function adequately as sources of social order, and legal compulsion insinuates itself into the growing gaps in natural restraint.

WILL DURANT (U.S. historian, 1885–1981)

History does not long entrust the care of freedom to the weak or the timid.

DWIGHT D. EISENHOWER (U.S. president, 1890–1969),
First Inaugural Address, January 20, 1953

For what avail the plough or sail,
Or land, or life, if freedom fail?

RALPH WALDO EMERSON (U.S.
philosopher, 1803–1882), "Boston"

NO LONGER VIRTUOUS NO LONGER FREE, is a maxim as true with regard to a private person as a commonwealth.

BENJAMIN FRANKLIN (U.S. printer, inventor, and statesman, 1706–1790), *Poor Richard's Almanack*

Liberty lies in the hearts of men and women; when it dies there, no constitution, no law, no court can save it.

LEARNED HAND (U.S. jurist, 1872–1961)

When we lose the right to be different, we lose the privilege to be free.

CHARLES EVANS HUGHES (U.S. Supreme Court chief justice, 1862–1948)

It seems to me perfectly in the cards that there will be within the next generation or so a pharmacological method of making people love their servitude, and producing . . . a kind of painless concentration camp for entire societies, so that people will in fact have their liberties taken away from them but will rather enjoy it, because they will be distracted from any desire to rebel by propaganda, brainwashing, or brainwashing enhanced by pharmacological methods.

ALDOUS HUXLEY (English writer, 1894–1963)

The history of the world shows that republics and democracies have generally lost their liberties by way of passing from civilian to quasi-military status. Nothing is more conducive to arbitrary rule than the military junta.

DOUGLAS MacARTHUR (U.S. general, 1880–1964)

IF A NATION VALUES ANYTHING MORE THAN FREE-DOM, IT WILL LOSE ITS FREEDOM; and the irony of it is that if it is comfort or money that it values more, it will lose that too.

W. SOMERSET MAUGHAM (English writer, 1874–1965)

In Germany they came first for the Communists, and I didn't speak up because I wasn't a Communist. Then they came for the Jews, and I didn't speak up because I wasn't a Jew. Then they came for the trade unionists, and I didn't speak up because I wasn't a trade unionist. Then they came for the Catholics, and I didn't speak up because I was a Protestant. Then they came for me, and by that time no one was left to speak up.

MARTIN NIEMÖLLER (German theologian, 1892–1984)

I would not be a king if I had to lose my liberty.

PHAEDRUS (Macedonian-born Roman writer
and emancipated slave, first century A.D.)

If you white men had never come here, this country would still be like it was. It would be all pure here. You call it wild, but it wasn't really wild, it was free. Animals aren't wild, they're just free. And that's the way we were. You called us wild, you called us savages. But we were just free!

LEON SHENANDOAH (contemporary U.S.
political leader, Iroquois Confederacy)

The saddest epitaph which can be carved in memory of a vanished liberty is that it was lost because its possessors failed to stretch forth a saving hand while yet there was time.

GEORGE SUTHERLAND (U.S. Supreme Court
associate justice, 1862–1942)

FREEDOM LOST, ALL LOST.

SAYING

freedom's
struggle

Not only to see and find the Divine in oneself, but to see and find the Divine in all, not only to seek one's own individual liberation and perfection, but to seek the liberation and perfection of others is the complete law of the spiritual being.

SRI AUROBINDO (Indian philosopher
and poet, 1872–1950)

The paradox of liberation is that in order to preserve freedom and to struggle for it, one must in a sense be already free, having freedom within oneself.

NICOLAS BERDYAEV (Russian
philosopher, 1874–1948)

None who have always been free can understand the terrible fascinating power of the hope of freedom to those who are not free.

PEARL BUCK (U.S. writer, 1892–1973)

The instinct of nearly all societies is to lock up anybody who is truly free. First, society begins by trying to beat you up. If this fails, they try to poison you. If this fails too, they finish by loading honors on your head.

JEAN COCTEAU (French poet, 1889–1963)

A liberation movement that is nonviolent sets the oppressor free as well as the oppressed.

BARBARA DEMING (U.S. writer and
human rights activist, 1917–1984)

Those who profess to love freedom and yet deprecate agitation are those who want crops without plowing. This struggle may be a moral one, or it may be physical, but it must be a struggle. Power concedes nothing without a demand. It never did, and it never will.

FREDERICK DOUGLASS (U.S. escaped slave,
abolitionist, and social reformer, 1817–1895)

Don't ask f'r rights. Take thim. An' don't let anny wan give thim to ye. A right that is handed to ye f'r nawthin' has somethin' th' matter with it.

PETER FINLEY DUNNE (U.S. writer and
humorist, 1867–1936)

Talkin' about [freedom] and bein' it, that's two different things. I mean it's real hard to be free when you're bought 'n' sold in the marketplace. **BUT DON' EVER TELL ANYBODY THAT THEY'RE NOT FREE, 'CAUSE THEN THEY GONNA GET TO KILLIN' AND MAIMIN' TO PROVE TO YOU THAT THEY ARE.** Oh yea, they gonna talk to you an' talk to ya an' talk to ya an' talk to ya about individual freedom, but if they see a free individual, it's gonna scare 'em.

PETER FONDA, DENNIS HOPPER, and TERRY SOUTHERN (contemporary U.S. actors and screenwriters), *Easy Rider* (film), 1969, spoken by Jack Nicholson

I walked lonely in the valley of the shadow of life. . . .

When midnight came and the spirits emerged from hidden places, i saw a cadaverous, dying specter fall to her knees, gazing at the moon. i approached her, asking, "What is your name?"

"My name is liberty," replied this ghastly shadow of a corpse.

And I inquired, "where are your children?"

And liberty, tearful and weak, gasped, "one died crucified, another died mad, and the third one is not yet born."

KAHLIL GIBRAN (Syrian poet, 1883–1931), "Between Night and Morning"

If a father does an injustice, it is the duty of his children to leave the parental roof. If the headmaster of a school conducts his institution on an immoral basis, the pupils must leave the school. If the chairman of a corporation is corrupt, the members thereof must wash their hands clean of his corruption by withdrawing from it; even so, if a government does a grave injustice, the subjects must withdraw cooperation wholly or partially, sufficiently to wean the ruler from his wickedness.

Freedom won through bloodshed or fraud is no freedom.

MOHANDAS K. GANDHI (Indian spiritual
and nationalist leader, 1869–1948)

I am not a liberator. Liberators do not exist. The people liberate themselves.

CHE GUEVARA (Argentinian revolutionary
leader, 1928–1967)

FREEDOM FIGHTERS DON'T ALWAYS WIN, BUT THEY ARE ALWAYS RIGHT.

MOLLY IVINS (contemporary U.S. journalist)

Exercise the right to dream. You must face reality—that which is; but then dream of the reality that ought to be—that must be. Live beyond the pain of reality with the dream of a bright tomorrow. Use hope and imagination as weapons of survival and progress. Use love to motivate you and obligate you to serve the human family.

JESSE JACKSON (contemporary U.S. human rights leader)

The desire to gain wealth and the fear to lose it are our chief breeders of cowardice and propagators of corruption. . . . Think of the strength which personal indifference to poverty would give us if we were devoted to unpopular causes. We need no longer hold our tongues or fear to vote the revolutionary or reformatory ticket. Our stocks might fall, our hopes of promotion vanish, our salaries stop, our club doors close in our faces; yet, while we lived, we would imperturbably bear witness to the spirit, and our example would help to set free our generation.

WILLIAM JAMES (U.S. physician, psychologist, and philosopher, 1842–1910)

We are not to expect to be translated from despotism to liberty in a featherbed.

THOMAS JEFFERSON (U.S. president, 1743–1826)

Let us not accept violence as the way to peace. Let us instead begin by respecting true freedom: The resulting peace will be able to satisfy the world's expectations; for it will be a peace built on justice, a peace founded on the incomparable dignity of the free human being.

JOHN PAUL II (contemporary Polish pope), World Peace Day message, January 1, 1981

The most powerful single force in the world today is neither communism nor capitalism, neither the H-bomb nor the guided missile—it is man's eternal desire to be free and independent.

JOHN F. KENNEDY (U.S. president, 1917–1963)

The nonviolent approach does not immediately change the heart of the oppressor. It first does something to the hearts and souls of those committed to it. It gives them new self-respect; it calls up resources of strength and courage that they did not know they had. Finally it reaches the opponent and so stirs his conscience that reconciliation becomes a reality.

———·———

Freedom is not given, it is won by struggle.

———·———

Man dies when he refuses to stand up for that which is right. A man dies when he refuses to take a stand for that which is true. So we are going to stand up right here . . . letting the world know we are determined to be free.

MARTIN LUTHER KING JR. (U.S. clergyman
and human rights leader, 1929–1968)

That is the truly beautiful and encouraging aspect of freedom; no one struggles for it just for himself.

ANNY LEWALD (German writer, 1811–1889)

The fight must go on. The cause of civil liberty must not be surrendered at the end of one or even one hundred defeats.

ABRAHAM LINCOLN (U.S. president, 1809–1865)

He only has known the full joy of living who somewhere and at some time has struck a decisive blow for the freedom of the human spirit.

WALTER LIPPMANN (U.S. journalist, 1889–1974)

MANY POLITICIANS OF OUR TIME ARE IN THE HABIT OF LAYING IT DOWN AS A SELF-EVIDENT PROPOSITION, THAT NO PEOPLE OUGHT TO BE FREE TILL THEY ARE FIT TO USE THEIR FREEDOM. THE MAXIM IS WORTHY OF THE FOOL IN THE OLD STORY, WHO RESOLVED NOT TO GO INTO THE WATER TILL HE HAD LEARNED TO SWIM. IF MEN ARE TO WAIT FOR LIBERTY TILL THEY BECOME WISE AND GOOD IN SLAVERY, THEY MAY INDEED WAIT FOREVER.

THOMAS BABINGTON MACAULAY
(English writer, 1800–1859)

Our objective is complete freedom, complete justice, complete equality—by any means necessary.

MALCOLM X (U.S. clergyman and
human rights leader, 1925–1965)

There is no easy walk to freedom.

To be free is not merely to cast off one's chains, but to live in a way that respects and enhances the freedom of others.

NELSON MANDELA (contemporary South African
president and human rights leader)

Get up, stand up
Stand up for your rights
Get up, stand up
Don't give up the fight!

BOB MARLEY (Jamaican songwriter
and singer, 1945–1981), "Get Up, Stand Up"

THE CRISIS

These are the times that try men's souls. The summer soldier and the sunshine patriot will, in this crisis, shrink from the service of his country; but he that stands it *now,* deserves the love and thanks of man and woman. Tyranny, like hell, is not easily conquered; yet we have this consolation with us, that the harder the conflict, the more glorious the triumph. What we obtain too cheap, we esteem too lightly: 'Tis dearness only that gives every thing its value. Heaven knows how to put a proper price upon its goods; and it would be strange indeed, if so celestial an article as FREEDOM should not be highly rated.

THOMAS PAINE (English-born U.S. political philosopher, 1737–1809), *The Crisis,* December 23, 1776

Proclaim liberty throughout the land to all the inhabitants.

> MOSES (Hebrew founder of Judaism,
> fourteenth century B.C.), *Leviticus* 25:10

HOW IS FREEDOM MEASURED, IN INDIVIDUALS AS IN NATIONS? BY THE RESISTANCE WHICH HAS TO BE OVERCOME.

FRIEDRICH NIETZSCHE (German philosopher, 1844–1900)

Those men and women are fortunate who are born at a time when a great struggle for human freedom is in progress.

> EMMELINE PANKHURST (English women's
> rights leader, 1858–1928)

Children's liberation is the next item on our civil rights shopping list.

> LETTY COTTIN POGREBIN (contemporary U.S. writer)

Freedom is never a final fact, but a continuing process to higher and higher levels of human, social, economic, political and religious relationships.

> A. PHILIP RANDOLPH (U.S.
> labor leader, 1889–1979)

It is of small importance to any of us whether we get liberty; but of the greatest that we deserve it. Whether we can win it, fate must determine; but that we will be worthy of it, we may ourselves determine; and the sorrowfullest fate, of all that we can suffer, is to have it without deserving it.

JOHN RUSKIN (English writer and art critic, 1819–1900)

There is a time when the operation of the machine becomes so odious, makes you so sick at heart that you can't take part; you can't even tacitly take part, and you've got to put your bodies upon the levers, upon all the apparatus, and you've got to make it stop. **AND YOU'VE GOT TO INDICATE TO THE PEOPLE WHO RUN IT, TO THE PEOPLE WHO OWN IT, THAT UNLESS YOU'RE FREE THE MACHINE WILL BE PREVENTED FROM WORKING AT ALL.**

MARIO SAVIO (U.S. student leader, 1942–1996),
University of California speech, Berkeley, 1964

Liberty, when it begins to take root, is a plant of rapid growth.

GEORGE WASHINGTON (U.S. president, 1732–1799)

THE MEANS WE USE TO STRUGGLE FOR JUSTICE, EVEN FOR REVOLUTIONARY CHANGE, MUST SCRUPULOUSLY OBSERVE HUMAN RIGHTS. The lives and liberties of ordinary people must not be sacrificed, either by governments or by revolutionaries, certain that they know the end results of what they do, or indifferent to their own ignorance.

HOWARD ZINN (contemporary U.S. historian)

If you're coming to help me, you are wasting your time. But if you have come because your liberation is bound up with mine, then let us work together.

ANONYMOUS (ABORIGINAL AUSTRALIAN)

I know one thing we did right
Was the day we started to fight,
Keep your eyes on the prize,
Hold on, hold on!
Freedom's name is mighty sweet
Black and white are gonna meet,
Keep your eyes on the prize,
Hold on, hold on!

ANONYMOUS (U.S.),
"Keep Your Eyes on the Prize" (song)

GOVERNMENT *government*

THE FINAL END OF EVERY POLITICAL INSTITUTION IS THE PRESERVATION OF THE NATURAL AND IMPRESCRIPTIBLE RIGHTS OF MAN.

These rights are those of liberty, property, security and resistance to oppression.

> DECLARATION OF THE RIGHTS OF MAN AND
> THE CITIZEN, France, Article 2, 1789

You don't need a lot of bureaucrats looking over your shoulder and telling you how to run your life or how to run your business. We are a people who declared our independence 200 years ago, and we are not about to lose it now to paper shufflers and computers.

> GERALD R. FORD (contemporary U.S. president)

Happy it is when the interest which the government has in the preservation of its own power, coincides with a proper distribution of the public burdens, and tends to guard the least wealthy part of the community from oppression!

> ALEXANDER HAMILTON (West Indian-born
> U.S. secretary of the treasury, 1755–1804),
> in *The Federalist Papers,* January 8, 1788

A wise and frugal government, which shall restrain men from injuring one another, shall leave them otherwise free to regulate their own pursuits of industry and improvement, and shall not take from the mouth of labor the bread it has earned. This is the sum of good government.

THOMAS JEFFERSON (U.S. president, 1743–1826),
First Inaugural Address, March 4, 1801

There is a zone of liberty . . . where the individual can tell the government, "Beyond this line you may not go."

ANTHONY M. KENNEDY (contemporary
U.S. Supreme Court associate justice)

All government and all private institutions must be designed to promote and protect and defend the integrity and the dignity of the individual. And that is the essential meaning of the Constitution and the Bill of Rights.

DAVID E. LILIENTHAL (U.S. public
administrator, 1899–1981)

Must a government, of necessity, be too strong for the liberties of its own people, or too weak to maintain its own existence?

ABRAHAM LINCOLN (U.S. president, 1809–1865)

'Tis not without reason that [man] seeks out and is willing to join in society with others who are already united or have a mind to unite for the mutual preservation of their lives, liberties and estates, which I call by the general name, property.

The great and chief end, therefore, of men's uniting into commonwealths, and putting themselves under government, is the preservation of their property.

JOHN LOCKE (English philosopher, 1632–1704),
Two Treatises of Government

In all the more advanced communities the great majority of things are worse done by the intervention of government than the individuals most interested in the matter would do them, or cause them to be done, if left to themselves.

JOHN STUART MILL (English philosopher, 1806–1873)

In proportion as you give the state power to do things *for* you, you give it power to do things *to* you.

ALBERT JAY NOCK (U.S. writer, 1870–1945)

I hope we have once again reminded people that man is not free unless government is limited. There's a clear cause and effect here that is as neat and predictable as a law of physics: as government expands, liberty contracts.

RONALD REAGAN (contemporary U.S. president),
farewell address, January 11, 1989

The object of government is not to change men from rational beings into beasts or puppets, but to enable them to develop their minds and bodies in security, and to employ their reason unshackled; neither showing hatred, anger or deceit, nor watched with the eyes of jealousy and injustice. In fact, the true aim of government is liberty.

BARUCH SPINOZA (Dutch philosopher, 1632–1677)

People are free in proportion as the state protects them from others; and are oppressed in proportion as the state protects them from *themselves.* "Look to the state for nothing beyond law and order," wrote Frederic Bastiat. "Count on it for no wealth, no enlightenment." Yet it is conventional wisdom today that we ought to look to the state for protection from drugs, mental illness, and suicide—in short, from our own choices and their consequences.

THOMAS S. SZASZ (contemporary
Hungarian-born U.S. psychiatrist)

The very idea of the power and the right of the people to establish government, presupposes the duty of every individual to obey the established government.

GEORGE WASHINGTON (U.S. president, 1732–1799),
Farewell Address, September 17, 1796

THE AMERICAN IDEA IS THAT GOVERNMENT EXISTS TO PROTECT, NOT TO GIVE, THE MOST FUNDAMENTAL RIGHTS which, as Jefferson wrote 220 July Fourths ago, are "inalienable" because they exist independent of, and prior to, government.

GEORGE F. WILL (contemporary U.S. journalist)

independence

I NOT ONLY HAVE THE RIGHT TO STAND UP FOR MYSELF, BUT I HAVE THE RESPONSI- BILITY. I can't ask somebody else to stand up for me if I won't standup for myself. And once you stand up for yourself, you'd be surprised that people say, "Can I be of help?"

MAYA ANGELOU (contemporary U.S. writer and poet)

I want the freedom to carve and chisel my own face, to staunch the bleeding with ashes, to fashion my own gods out of my entrails.

GLORIA ANZALDÚA (contemporary
Tejana Chicana poet)

SELF-SUFFICIENCY . . . HAS THREE MEANINGS. The first is that one should not depend upon others for one's daily bread. The second is that one should have developed the power to acquire knowledge for oneself. The third is that a man should be able to rule himself, to control his senses and his thoughts.

VINOBA BHAVE (Indian social reformer, 1895–1982)

I have a sense of going my own way, and I don't really think much about whether it's going against the grain. I don't really want to spend a lot of time worrying about how I am perceived by other people.

KATHLEEN COLLINS (U.S. filmmaker, 1931–1988)

Where the way is hardest, there go thou:
Follow your own path, and let people talk.

DANTE ALIGHIERI (Italian poet, 1265–1321),
The Divine Comedy, "Purgatory"

To free us from the expectations of others, to give us back to ourselves—there lies the great, singular power of self-respect.

JOAN DIDION (contemporary U.S. writer)

Whoso goes to walk alone, accuses the whole world; he declareth all to be unfit to be his companions; it is very uncivil, nay, insulting; Society will retaliate.

I must be myself. I cannot break myself anymore for you. . . . I cannot sell liberty and my power to save their sensibility.

When I was introduced to [Abraham Lincoln], he said, "Oh Mr. Emerson, I once heard you say in a lecture that a Kentuckian seems to say by his air and manners, 'Here I am; if you don't like me, the worse for you.'" (referring to an 1862 meeting in Washington, D.C., with the Kentucky-born president, who "impressed me more favorably than I had hoped")

RALPH WALDO EMERSON
(U.S. philosopher, 1803–1882)

Is freedom anything else than the power of living as we choose?

> EPICTETUS (Greek philosopher, first century A.D.)

I shall be telling this with a sigh
Somewhere ages and ages hence:
Two roads diverged in a wood, and I-
I took the one less traveled by,
And that has made all the difference.

I hold it to be the inalienable right of anybody to go to hell in his own way.

> ROBERT FROST (U.S. poet, 1874–1963),

The path toward self-sufficiency is the never-finished process of realizing one's full human potential in the context of community. It is a path from dependence through relative independence to a conscious and active state of interdependence.

> GREYSTON BAKERY (Yonkers, New York),
> "Mission Statement and Principles," 1999

Most people are like a falling leaf that drifts and turns in the air, flutters, and falls to the ground. But a few others are like stars which travel one defined path: no wind reaches them, they have within themselves their guide and path.

HERMANN HESSE (German writer, 1877–1962)

It's easy to be independent when you've got money. But to be independent when you haven't got a thing— that's the Lord's test.

MAHALIA JACKSON (U.S. singer, 1911–1972)

Freedom to differ is not limited to things that do not matter much. That would be a mere shadow of freedom. The test of its substance is the right to differ as to things that touch the heart of the existing order.

ROBERT H. JACKSON (U.S. Supreme Court associate justice, 1892–1954), *West Virginia State Board of Education v. Barnette,* 1943

Conformity is the jailer of freedom and the enemy of growth.

JOHN F. KENNEDY (U.S. president, 1917–1963)

Neither the clamor of the mob nor the voice of power will ever turn me by the breadth of a hair from the course I mark out for myself guided by such knowledge as I can obtain, and controlled and directed by a solemn conviction of right and duty.

ROBERT M. La FOLLETTE (Wisconsin senator, 1855–1925)

I desire so to conduct the affairs of this administration that if at the end, when I come to lay down the reins of power, I have lost every other friend on earth, I shall at least have one friend left, and that friend shall be down inside of me.

ABRAHAM LINCOLN (U.S. president, 1809–1865)

I'm tough, I'm ambitious, and I know exactly what I want. If that makes me a bitch, okay.

MADONNA (contemporary U.S. singer and actor)

Human dignity . . . is derived from a sense of independence.

MARIA MONTESSORI (Italian physician
and educator, 1870–1952)

The essence of a free life is being able to choose the style of living you prefer free from exclusion and without the compulsion of conformity or law.

ELEANOR HOLMES NORTON (contemporary District of Columbia congresswoman)

We live in an age in which the autonomous individual is ceasing to exist—or perhaps one ought to say, in which the individual is ceasing to have the illusion of being autonomous.

GEORGE ORWELL (English writer, 1903–1950)

To conquer fortune and everything else, begin by independence.

JEAN-JACQUES ROUSSEAU (French philosopher, 1712–1778)

Only those who have helped themselves know how to help others, and to respect their right to help themselves.

People are always blaming their circumstances for what they are. I don't believe in circumstances. The people who get on in this world are the people who get up and look for the circumstances they want, and, if they don't find them, make them.

GEORGE BERNARD SHAW (British playwright and critic, 1856–1950)

In a free country every feller ought to cut his own fodder.

ANN SOPHIA STEPHENS (U.S. writer, 1813–1886)

Achieving dignity and individuality is always a personal affair. It can be facilitated or hindered; but, in the end, each person must do it for himself.

THOMAS S. SZASZ (contemporary Hungarian-born U.S. psychiatrist)

I WAS NOT BORN TO BE FORCED. I WILL BREATHE AFTER MY OWN FASHION. . . . IF A PLANT CANNOT LIVE ACCORDING TO ITS NATURE, IT DIES; AND SO A MAN.

———•———

I would not have anyone adopt my mode of living. . . . I desire that there may be as many different persons in the world as possible; but I would have each one be very careful to find out and pursue his own way, and not his father's or his mother's or his neighbor's instead.

———•———

Why should we be in such desperate haste to succeed, and in such desperate enterprises? If a man does not keep pace with his companions, perhaps it is because he hears a different drummer. Let him step to the music that he hears, however measured or far away.

HENRY DAVID THOREAU
(U.S. philosopher, 1817–1862)

THE MASTER IS HIS OWN PATH.

TUAN-MU TZ'U (Chinese sage, fifth century B.C.)

Integrity and firmness are all I can promise. These, be the voyage long or short, shall never forsake me, although I may be deserted by all men; for of the consolations, which are to be derived from these, under any circumstances, the world cannot deprive me.

GEORGE WASHINGTON (U.S. president, 1732–1799),
four weeks before assuming the presidency in 1789

What is independence? Freedom from all laws or bonds except those of one's own being, control'd by the universal ones.

WALT WHITMAN (U.S. poet, 1819–1892)

Independence I have long considered as the grand blessing of life, the basis of every virtue.

HOW CAN A RATIONAL BEING BE ENNOBLED BY ANYTHING THAT IS NOT OBTAINED BY ITS OWN EXERTIONS?

MARY WOLLSTONECRAFT (English writer, 1759–1797), *A Vindication of the Rights of Woman*

The man who is aware of himself is henceforward independent, and he is never bored, and life is only too short, and he is steeped through and through with a profound yet temperate happiness. He alone lives, while other people, slaves of ceremony, let life slip past them in a kind of dream.

VIRGINIA WOOLF (English writer, 1882–1941)

This man is free from servile bands,
    Of hope to rise, or fear to fall:
Lord of himself, though not of lands,
    And, have nothing, yet hath all.

SIR HENRY WOTTON (English diplomat and poet, 1568–1639), "The Character of a Happy Life"

the **individual**

ALL THAT IS VALUABLE IN HUMAN SOCIETY DEPENDS UPON THE OPPORTUNITY FOR DEVELOPMENT ACCORDED TO THE INDIVIDUAL.

ALBERT EINSTEIN (German-born
U.S. physicist, 1879–1955)

The first individual was a lone survivor, a straggler, an outcast, a fugitive. Individual selfhood was first experienced not as something ardently wished for but as a calamity which befell the individual: he was separated from the group. All creative phases in history were preceded by a shattering or weakening of communal structures, and it was the individual debris who first set the creative act in motion.

ERIC HOFFER (U.S. longshoreman
and philosopher, 1902–1983)

Even in exceptional situations that may at times arise, one can never justify any violation of the fundamental dignity of the human person or of the basic rights that safeguard this dignity.

JOHN PAUL II (contemporary Polish pope)

At the heart of . . . western freedom and democracy is the belief that the individual man, the child of God, is the touchstone of value, and all society, groups, the state, exist for his benefit. Therefore the enlargement of liberty for individual human beings must be the supreme goal and the abiding practice of any western society.

ROBERT F. KENNEDY (U.S. attorney general
and New York senator, 1925–1968)

I believe each individual is naturally entitled to do as he pleases with himself and the fruit of his labor, so far as it in no [way] interferes with any other man's rights.

ABRAHAM LINCOLN (U.S. president, 1809–1865)

ON LIBERTY

The liberty of the individual must be thus far limited; he must not make himself a nuisance to other people.

———

The sole end for which mankind are warranted, individually or collectively, in interfering with the liberty of action of any of their number, is self-protection. That the only purpose for which power can be rightfully exercised over any member of a civilized community, against his will, is to prevent harm to others. His own good, either physical or moral, is not a sufficient warrant.

———

The individual is not accountable to society for his actions in so far as these concern the interests of no person but himself. Advice, instruction, persuasion, and avoidance by other people, if thought necessary by them for their own good, are the only measures by which society can justifiably express its dislike or disapprobation of his conduct.

To extend the bounds of what may be called moral police until it encroaches on the most unquestionably legitimate liberty of the individual is one of the most universal of all human propensities.

JOHN STUART MILL
(English philosopher, 1806–1873), *On Liberty,* 1859

Freedom is the recognition that no single person, no single authority or government has a monopoly on truth, but that every individual life is infinitely precious, that every one of us put in this world has been put here for a reason and has something to offer.

RONALD REAGAN (contemporary U.S. president)

There will never be a really free and enlightened state until the state comes to recognize the individual as a higher and independent power, from which all its own power and authority are derived, and treats him accordingly.

HENRY DAVID THOREAU (U.S. philosopher, 1817–1862)

WHEN ONE MAN SAYS, "NO, I WON'T," ROME BEGINS TO FEAR.

DALTON TRUMBO (U.S. screenwriter, 1905–1976),
Spartacus (film), 1960, spoken by Kirk Douglas

The individual is indisputably the original, the first fact of liberty. . . . There is no such thing as corporate liberty. Liberty belongs to the individual, or it does not exist.

WOODROW WILSON (U.S. president, 1856–1924)

JUSTICE *justice*

To practice justice is to practice liberty.

SIMON BOLÍVAR (South American statesman, 1783–1830)

Whenever a separation is made between liberty and justice, neither is . . . safe.

EDMUND BURKE (British statesman
and philosopher, 1729–1797)

Justice, though due to the accused, is due to the accuser also.

BENJAMIN N. CARDOZO (U.S. Supreme Court
associate justice, 1870–1938)

The mood and temper of the public in regard to the treatment of crime and criminals is one of the most unfailing tests of the civilization of any country. A calm, dispassionate recognition of the rights of the accused, and even of the convicted criminal, . . . measures the stored-up strength of a nation and [is] sign and proof of the living virtue in it.

WINSTON CHURCHILL (British prime minister, 1874–1965)

[A year after the horrifying events of September 11, 2001] with the exception of the right to bear arms, one would be hard pressed to name a single constitutional liberty that the Bush Administration has not overridden in the name of protecting our freedom. Privacy has given way to Internet tracking. . . . Physical liberty and habeas corpus survive only until the President decides someone is a "bad guy." Property is seized without notice, without a hearing and on the basis of secret evidence. Equal protection has fallen prey to ethnic profiling. Conversations with a lawyer may be monitored without a warrant or denied altogether when the military finds them inconvenient. And the right to a public hearing upon arrest exists only at the Attorney General's sufferance.

DAVID COLE (contemporary U.S. journalist)

The privilege of the writ of habeas corpus shall not be suspended, unless when in cases of rebellion or invasion the public safety may require it.

CONSTITUTION OF THE UNITED STATES,
Article 1, Section 9, 1789

CONSTITUTION OF THE UNITED STATES
EXCERPTS FROM THE BILL OF RIGHTS

No person shall be . . . subject for the same offense to be twice put in jeopardy of life or limb; nor shall be compelled in any criminal case to be a witness against himself, nor be deprived of life, liberty or property, without due process of law.

Fifth Amendment, 1791

In all criminal prosecutions, the accused shall enjoy the right to a speedy and public trial, by an impartial jury of the State and district wherein the crime shall have been committed, . . . and to be informed of the nature and cause of the accusation; to be confronted with the witnesses against him; to have compulsory process for obtaining witnesses in his favor; and to have the assistance of counsel for his defense.

Sixth Amendment, 1791

Excessive bail shall not be required, nor excessive fines imposed, nor cruel and unusual punishments inflicted.

Eighth Amendment, 1791

The Fifth Amendment [which protects the accused from being forced to bear witness against himself] is an old friend, and a good one. It is one of the great landmarks in man's struggle to be free of tyranny, to be decent and civilized. It is our way to escape torture. It protects man against any form of Inquisition. It is part of our respect for the dignity of man.

> WILLIAM O. DOUGLAS (U.S. Supreme Court
> associate justice, 1898–1980)

The history of liberty has largely been the history of observance of procedural safeguards.

> FELIX FRANKFURTER (U.S. Supreme Court
> associate justice, 1882–1965)

We have to choose, and for my part I think it a less evil that some criminals should escape than that the government should play an ignoble part.

> OLIVER WENDELL HOLMES JR. (U.S. Supreme Court chief
> justice, 1841–1935), *Olmstead v. United States,* 1928

Justice is indiscriminately due to all, without regard to numbers, wealth, or rank.

> JOHN JAY (U.S. Supreme Court chief justice, 1745–1829)

The justice of a social and economic system is finally measured by the way in which a person's work is rewarded. . . . A just wage is a concrete measure, and in a sense the key one, of the justice of a system.

JOHN PAUL II (contemporary Polish pope)

In a free society the state does not administer the affairs of men. It administers justice among men who conduct their own affairs.

WALTER LIPPMANN (U.S. journalist, 1889–1974)

To no one will we sell, to no one will we deny or delay right or justice.

MAGNA CHARTA (English charter of rights, 1215)

ANONYMOUS: **HOW CAN JUSTICE BE SECURED IN ATHENS?**

SOLON: **IF THOSE WHO ARE NOT INJURED FEEL AS INDIGNANT AS THOSE WHO ARE.**

SOLON (Greek statesman, sixth century B.C.)

[In *Miranda v. Arizona* (1966), the U.S. Supreme Court] required police to advise criminal suspects of particular constitutional rights prior to interrogation. These Miranda warnings consisted of four items: (1) the right to remain silent; (2) the reminder that anything said could be used against the suspect; (3) the right to counsel; and (4) the related reminder that counsel would be provided for indigents.

SUZETTE M. TALARICO (contemporary
U.S. political scientist)

I hope Americans are as appalled as I am by reports that we are abusing suspected al Qaeda terrorists in secret CIA interrogation centers overseas. Last week The Washington Post detailed a "brass-knuckled quest for information, often in concert with allies of dubious human rights reputation." Those who refuse to cooperate are deprived of sleep and are kept standing or held in other painful positions for hours. Some are turned over to foreign intelligence services known for more horrific torture.

Is this really us? Is this type of treatment going to win friends around the world?

HELEN THOMAS (contemporary U.S.
journalist), January 4, 2003

The right to silence is more than the mere right to refuse to answer incriminating questions. It is the respect which society pays to the inviolability of each man's soul in an era when hypnotism, narco-analysis, truth serums, lie detectors and other scientific devices are being used to force the revelation of truths by persons who desire to keep them secret. . . . It is a last bastion against an ever more omnipotent government. It is the final shield against invasion of the soul. Protection from this kind of assault is the sine qua non of the essential dignity of man.

EDWARD BENNETT WILLIAMS (U.S. lawyer, 1920–1988)

JUSTICE THE GUARDIAN OF LIBERTY.

ANONYMOUS, inscription on the East Portico of the U.S. Supreme Court Building in Washington, D.C.

law

Our liberty, wisely understood, is but a voluntary obedience to the universal laws of life.

HENRI AMIEL (Swiss poet and philosopher, 1821–1881)

The law has progressed to the point where we should declare that the punishment of death, like punishment on the rack, the screw, and the wheel, is no longer morally tolerable.

WILLIAM J. BRENNAN JR. (U.S. Supreme Court associate justice, 1906–1997)

No State shall . . . deprive any person of life, liberty, or property, without due process of law; nor deny to any person under its jurisdiction equal protection of the law.

CONSTITUTION OF THE UNITED STATES, Fourteenth Amendment, 1868

We cannot expect to breed respect for law and order among people who do not share the fruits of our freedom.

HUBERT H. HUMPHREY (Minnesota senator and U.S. vice president, 1911–1978)

A strict observance of the written laws is doubtless one of the high duties of a good citizen, but it is not the highest. The laws of necessity, of self-preservation, of saving our country when in danger, are of higher obligation. To lose our country by a scrupulous adherence to written law, would be to lose the law itself, with life, liberty, property and all those who are enjoying them with us; thus absurdly sacrificing the end to the means.

THOMAS JEFFERSON (U.S. president, 1743–1826)

An individual who breaks a law that conscience tells him is unjust, and willingly accepts the penalty by staying in jail to arouse the conscience of the community over its injustice, is in reality expressing the very highest respect for law.

MARTIN LUTHER KING JR. (U.S. clergyman and
human rights leader, 1929–1968),
"Letter from Birmingham City Jail," April 16, 1963

THERE CAN BE NO LIBERTY WITHOUT LAW.

JOHN LOCKE (English philosopher, 1632–1704)

The very essence of civil liberty is the right of every individual to claim the protection of the laws whenever he receives an injury.

JOHN MARSHALL (U.S. Supreme Court chief justice, 1755–1835), *Marbury v. Madison,* 1803

The laws do not . . . punish anything other than overt acts.

MONTESQUIEU (French philosopher, 1689–1755)

Equal protection of the laws is something more than an abstract right. It is a command which the State must respect, the benefits of which every person may demand. Not the least merit of our constitutional system is that its safeguards extend to all—the least deserving as well as the most virtuous.

HARLAN F. STONE (U.S. Supreme Court chief justice, 1872–1946)

The shallow . . . consider
liberty a release from all law,
from every constraint.
The wise see in it, on the
contrary, the potent
Law of Laws . . . those
universal, eternal,
unconscious ones which run
through all Time, pervade
history, prove immortality,
give moral purpose to the
entire objective world,
and the last dignity
to human life.

WALT WHITMAN (U.S. poet, 1819–1892)

LIBERTY OR DEATH

Chains or conquest, liberty or death.

JOSEPH ADDISON (English writer, 1672–1719)

LIBERTY'S IN EVERY BLOW!
LET US DO OR DIE!

ROBERT BURNS (Scottish poet,
1759–1796), "Scots Wha Hae"

Is life so dear or peace so sweet, as to be purchased at the price of chains and slavery? Forbid it, Almighty God! I know not what course others may take, but as for me, give me liberty or give me death!

PATRICK HENRY (U.S. statesman, 1736–1799)

It is better to die on your feet than to live on your knees!

DOLORES IBÁRRURI (Spanish journalist and revolutionary leader, known as La Pasionaria, 1895–1989), radio broadcast from Paris during the Spanish Civil War urging the people of Spain to defend the Republic against the Fascist uprising, September 3, 1936

We most solemnly, before God and the world, declare, that, exerting the utmost energy of those powers, which our beneficent Creator hath graciously bestowed upon us, the arms we have been compelled by our enemies to assume, we will, in defiance of every hazard, with unabating firmness and perseverance, employ for the preservation of our liberties; being with one mind resolved to die free men rather than to live slaves.

THOMAS JEFFERSON (U.S. president, 1743–1826) and JOHN DICKINSON (U.S. political leader, 1732–1808), Declaration of the Causes and Necessity of Taking up Arms, July 6, 1776

Choosing to die resisting, rather than to live submitting, they fled only from dishonor, but met danger face to face.

PERICLES (Greek statesman, fifth century B.C.),
Funeral Oration, 431 B.C.

MORE THAN LIFE, I CHERISH FREEDOM.

FRIEDRICH von SCHILLER (German
playwright, 1759–1805)

O men of Athens . . . either acquit me or not; but whichever you do, understand that I shall never alter my ways, not even if I have to die many times.

> SOCRATES (Greek philosopher, fifth century B.C.)

I had started with this idea in my head, "Dere's two things I've got a right to, and dese are, Death or Liberty—one or tother I mean to have. No one will take me back alive."

> HARRIET TUBMAN (U.S. emancipated slave and abolitionist, 1820–1913)

THEY MAY TAKE OUR LIVES, BUT THEY'LL NEVER TAKE OUR FREEDOM.

RANDALL WALLACE (contemporary U.S. screenwriter), *Braveheart* (film), 1995, spoken by Mel Gibson (in the role of the Scottish rebel warrior William Wallace) to his troops before a battle

Live free or die.

STATE MOTTO (NEW HAMPSHIRE)

the **mind**

OF ALL THE TYRANNIES ON HUMANKIND, THE WORST IS THAT WHICH PERSECUTES THE MIND.

JOHN DRYDEN (English poet, 1631–1700),
The Hind and the Panther

Nothing is at last sacred but the integrity of your own mind.

RALPH WALDO EMERSON (U.S.
philosopher, 1803–1882)

He who endeavors to control the mind by force is a tyrant, and he who submits is a slave.

ROBERT G. INGERSOLL (U.S. lawyer
and lecturer, 1833–1899)

It is hard to fight an enemy who has outposts in your head.

SALLY KEMPTON (contemporary U.S. writer)

Almighty God hath created the mind free, and manifested his supreme will that free it shall remain by making it altogether insusceptible of restraint; . . . all attempts to influence it by temporal punishments, or burdens, or by civil incapacitations, tend only to beget habits of hypocrisy and meanness, and are a departure from the plan of the holy author of our religion, who being lord both of body and mind, yet chose not to propagate it by coercions on either, as was in his Almighty power to do, but to extend it by its influence on reason alone.

I have sworn upon the altar of God, eternal hostility against every form of tyranny over the mind of man.

THOMAS JEFFERSON (U.S. president, 1743–1826)

A study of the history of opinion is a necessary preliminary to the emancipation of the mind.

JOHN MAYNARD KEYNES (English
economist, 1883–1946)

YOU TELL ME IT'S THE INSTITUTION. WELL, YOU KNOW, YOU BETTER FREE YOUR MIND INSTEAD.

JOHN LENNON and PAUL McCARTNEY (contemporary English songwriters and singers), "Revolution"

Emancipate yourselves from mental slavery.
None but ourselves can free our minds.

BOB MARLEY (Jamaican songwriter and singer, 1945–1981), "Redemption Song"

Our whole constitutional heritage rebels at the thought of giving government the power to control men's minds.

THURGOOD MARSHALL (U.S. Supreme Court associate justice, 1908–1993)

What other liberty is there worth having, if we have not freedom and peace in our minds?

HENRY DAVID THOREAU (U.S. philosopher, 1817–1862)

the **press**

Congress shall make no law . . . abridging the freedom
. . . of the press.

CONSTITUTION OF THE UNITED STATES,
Bill of Rights, First Amendment, 1791

Acceptance by government of a dissident press is a measure of the maturity of a nation.

WILLIAM O. DOUGLAS (U.S. Supreme Court
associate justice, 1898–1980)

Wherever books are burned, sooner or later men also
are burned.

HEINRICH HEINE (German poet, 1797–1856)

To prohibit the reading of certain books is to declare the
inhabitants to be either fools or slaves.

CLAUDE-ADRIEN HELVÉTIUS (French
philosopher, 1715–1771)

Every president should have the right to shoot two reporters a year—without explanation.

HERBERT HOOVER (U.S. president, 1874–1964)

Our liberty depends on the freedom of the press, and that cannot be limited without being lost.

Were it left to me to decide whether we should have a government without newspapers, or newspapers without a government, I should not hesitate a moment to prefer the latter.

THOMAS JEFFERSON (U.S. president, 1743–1826)

If nothing may be published but what civil authority shall have previously approved, power must always be the standard of truth.

SAMUEL JOHNSON (English writer and lexicographer, 1709–1784)

The freedom of the press works in such a way that there is not much freedom from it.

GRACE KELLY (U.S.-born actor and
princess of Monaco, 1928–1982)

Why should freedom of speech and freedom of the press by allowed? Why should a government which is doing what it believes to be right allow itself to be criticized? It would not allow opposition by lethal weapons. Ideas are much more fatal things than guns. Why should any man be allowed to buy a printing press and disseminate pernicious opinions calculated to embarrass the government?

VLADIMIR LENIN (Russian revolutionary
leader, 1870–1924)

Freedom of the press is guaranteed only to those who own one.

A. J. LIEBLING (U.S. journalist, 1904–1963)

A press monopoly is incompatible with a free press; and one can proceed with this principle: if there is a monopoly of the means of communications—of radio, television, magazines, books, public meetings—it follows that this society is by definition and in fact deprived of freedom.

WALTER LIPPMANN (U.S. journalist, 1889–1974)

The press of Italy is free, freer than the press of any other country, so long as it supports the regime.

BENITO MUSSOLINI (Italian dictator, 1883–1945)

If I were to give liberty to the press, my power could not last three days.

NAPOLÉON BONAPARTE (French general and emperor, 1769–1821)

IT IS VERY DIFFICULT TO HAVE A FREE, FAIR AND HONEST PRESS ANYWHERE IN THE WORLD. In the first place, as a rule, papers are largely supported by advertising, and that immediately gives the advertisers a certain hold over the medium which they use.

ELEANOR ROOSEVELT (U.S. first lady and UN delegate, 1884–1962)

Freedom of the press is to the machinery of the state what the safety valve is to the steam engine.

ARTHUR SCHOPENHAUER (German
philosopher, 1788–1860)

Woe to that nation whose literature is cut short by the intrusion of force. This is not merely interference with "freedom of the press" but the sealing up of a nation's heart, the excision of its memory.

ALEKSANDR SOLZHENITSYN
(contemporary Russian writer)

THE PRESS TODAY IS AN ARMY WITH CAREFULLY ORGANIZED ARMS AND BRANCHES, WITH JOURNAL-ISTS AS OFFICERS, AND READERS AS SOLDIERS. But here, as in every army, the soldier obeys blindly, and war aims and operation plans change without his knowledge. The reader neither knows, nor is allowed to know, the purposes for which he is used, nor even the role that he is to play. A more appalling caricature of freedom of thought cannot be imagined.

OSWALD SPENGLER (German historian, 1880–1936)

The rock-bottom foundation of a free press is the integrity of the people who run it.

ADLAI E. STEVENSON (Illinois governor, presidential candidate and UN ambassador, 1900–1965)

Freedom of the press in Britain means freedom to print such of the proprietor's prejudices as the advertisers don't object to.

HANNEN SWAFFER (British journalist, 1879–1962)

The press is the chief democratic instrument of freedom.

ALEXIS de TOCQUEVILLE (French statesman and writer, 1805–1859)

I can imagine no greater disservice to the country than to establish a system of censorship that would deny to the people of a free republic like our own their indisputable right to criticize their own public officials. While exercising the great powers of the office I hold, I would regret in a crisis like the one through which we are now passing to lose the benefit of patriotic and intelligent criticism.

WOODROW WILSON (U.S. president, 1856–1924), three weeks after the United States entered World War I, letter to Arthur Brisbane, April 25, 1917

privacy

The world, the state, the church, the school, all are felons whensoever they violate the sanctity of the private human heart.

BRONSON ALCOTT (U.S. teacher and writer, 1799–1888)

What is surprising is that so many ordinary American citizens tolerate without protest the most shameless invasion of their privacy. . . .

A man's sex life, political views and childhood relationship with his mother are his own business, and nobody else's. The proper response about such matters is a loud, positive: "IT'S NONE OF YOUR LOUSY BUSINESS."

STEWART ALSOP (U.S. journalist, 1914–1974)

A freedom to determine the extent to which others may share in one's spiritual nature, and the ability to protect one's beliefs, thoughts, emotions, and sensations from unreasonable intrusions are of the very essence of life in a free society.

WILLIAM BEANEY (contemporary U.S. professor of law)

The right of an individual to conduct intimate relationships in the intimacy of his or her own home seems to me to be the heart of the Constitution's protection of privacy. . . .

[Disapproval of homosexuality cannot justify] invading the houses, hearts and minds of citizens who choose to live their lives differently.

HARRY A. BLACKMUN (U.S. Supreme Court associate justice, 1908–1999)

A MAN ALWAYS IS TO BE HIMSELF THE JUDGE HOW MUCH OF HIS MIND HE WILL SHOW TO OTHER MEN; even to those he would have work along with him. There are impertinent inquiries made: your rule is, to leave the inquirer uninformed on that matter; not, if you can help it, misinformed; but precisely as dark as he was!

THOMAS CARLYLE (English historian, 1795–1881)

The makers of our Constitution undertook to secure conditions favorable to the pursuit of happiness. They recognized the significance of man's spiritual nature, of his feelings and of his intellect. They knew that only a part of the pain, pleasure and satisfactions of life are to be found in material things. They sought to protect Americans in their beliefs, their thoughts, their emotions and their sensations. They conferred, as against the Government, the right to be let alone-the most comprehensive of rights and the right most valued by civilized men.

LOUIS D. BRANDEIS (U.S. Supreme Court associate justice, 1856–1941), *Olmstead v. United States,* 1928

The right of the people to be secure in their persons, houses, papers, and effects, against unreasonable searches and seizures, shall not be violated, and no warrants shall issue but upon probable cause, supported by oath or affirmation, and particularly describing the place to be searched, and the persons or things to be seized.

CONSTITUTION OF THE UNITED STATES, Bill of Rights, Fourth Amendment, 1791

Don't put no constrictions on da people. Leave 'em to hell alone.

JIMMY DURANTE (U.S. entertainer, 1893–1980)

THE BASIC TEST OF FREEDOM IS PERHAPS LESS IN WHAT WE ARE FREE TO DO THAN IN WHAT WE ARE FREE NOT TO DO. It is the freedom to refrain, withdraw and abstain which makes a totalitarian regime impossible.

ERIC HOFFER (U.S. longshoreman
and philosopher, 1902–1983)

If the First Amendment means anything, it means that a State has no business telling a man, sitting alone in his own house, what books he may read or what films he may watch.

THURGOOD MARSHALL (U.S. Supreme Court
associate justice, 1908–1993)

Who could deny that privacy is a jewel? It has always been the mark of privilege, the distinguishing feature of a truly urbane culture. Out of the cave, the tribal teepee, the pueblo, the community fortress, man emerged to build himself a house of his own with a shelter in it for himself and his diversions. Every age has seen it so. The poor might have to huddle together in cities for need's sake, and the frontiersman cling to his neighbors for the sake of protection. But in each civilization, as it advanced, those who could afford it chose the luxury of a withdrawing-place.

PHYLLIS McGINLEY (U.S. poet, 1905–1978)

People have a right to their own lives, and if you can't help somebody, you ought to get out of their way.

KATE MILLET (contemporary U.S. writer)

In their vigorous advocacy of the public's right to know, the media frequently violate a right that has a higher standing—the individual's right to privacy.

RICHARD M. NIXON (U.S. president, 1913–1994)

A man has a right to pass through this world, if he wills, without having his picture published, his business enterprises discussed, his successful experiments written up for the benefit of others, or his eccentricities commented upon, whether in handbills, circulars, catalogues, newspapers or periodicals.

ALTON B. PARKER (U.S. jurist, 1852–1926)

The poorest man may in his cottage bid defiance to all the forces of the Crown. It may be frail—its roof may shake—the wind may blow through it—the storm may enter—the rain may enter–but the King of England cannot enter!—all his forces dare not cross the threshold of the ruined tenement!

WILLIAM PITT the ELDER (English prime minister, 1708–1778)

Just as it is illicit to appropriate another's goods or to make an attempt on his bodily integrity without his consent, so it is not permissible to enter into his inner domain against his will, whatever the technique or method used.

PIUS XII (Italian pope, 1876–1958)

In denying the government [the power to carry out warrantless wiretaps during Vietnam war protests], the Supreme Court quoted an observation from Chief Justice Earl Warren that has obvious relevance today. **"IT WOULD INDEED BE IRONIC IF, IN THE NAME OF NATIONAL DEFENSE, WE WOULD SANCTION THE SUBVERSION OF ONE OF THOSE LIBERTIES . . . WHICH MAKE THE DEFENSE OF THE NATION WORTHWHILE."**

DEBORAH L. RHODE (contemporary
U.S. journalist), 2002

The pretension of man to explore the conscience of others, the forcible rape of secrecy, are a diabolical parody of the all-seeingness of God.

JEAN ROLIN (contemporary French writer)

[Under the Homeland Security Act of 2002] here is what will happen to you: Every purchase you make with a credit card, every magazine subscription you buy and medical prescription you fill, every Web site you visit and e-mail you send or receive, every academic grade you receive, every bank deposit you make, every trip you book and every event you attend—all these transactions and communications will go into what the Defense Department describes as "a virtual, centralized grand database."

To this computerized dossier on your private life from commercial sources, add every piece of information that government has about you—assport application, driver's license and bridge toll records, judicial and divorce records, complaints from nosy neighbors to the F.B.I., your lifetime paper trail plus the latest hidden camera surveillance—and you have the supersnoop's dream: a "Total Information Awareness" about every U.S. citizen.

WILLIAM SAFIRE (contemporary U.S. journalist)

The electronic computer is to individual privacy what the machine gun was to the horse cavalry.

ALAN W. SCHEFLIN and EDWARD M. OPTON JR.
(contemporary U.S. lawyers)

The authority of any governing institution must stop at its citizen's skin.

GLORIA STEINEM (contemporary U.S. women's rights leader and writer)

The Fourth Amendment and the personal rights which it secures have a long history. At the very core stands the right of a man to retreat into his own home and there be free from unreasonable governmental intrusion.

POTTER STEWART (U.S. Supreme Court associate justice, 1915–1985)

RELIGION
religion

No one, no, not no one million
ones dare deny my God. I go forth
alone, and stand as ten thousand,

The Divine upon my right
impels me to pull forever
at the latch on Freedom's gate.

MAYA ANGELOU (contemporary U.S. writer and poet)

It is not an accident that freedom of religion is one of the central freedoms in our Bill of Rights. It is the first freedom of the human soul, the right to speak the words that God places in our mouths.

GEORGE W. BUSH (contemporary U.S. president)

The Americans who framed our Constitution felt that without freedom of religion no other freedom counted.

HENRY STEELE COMMAGER
(contemporary U.S. historian)

Congress shall make no law respecting an establishment of religion, or prohibiting the free exercise thereof.

CONSTITUTION OF THE UNITED STATES,
Bill of Rights, First Amendment, 1791

Religious liberty is the great contribution this nation has made to the world in both the realm of politics and religion.

———

I believe in a wall between church and state so high that no one can climb over it. When religion controls government, political liberty dies; and when government controls religion, religious liberty perishes.

———

If religious freedom is to endure in America, the responsibility for teaching religion to public school children must be left to the homes and churches of our land, where this responsibility rightfully belongs. It must not be assumed by the government through the agency of the public school system.

SAM J. ERVIN (North Carolina senator, 1896–1985)

Inside each of us, inside me, inside you, there is this kernel, or core, of something sacred, something that cannot be violated, something that cannot be coerced, or tampered with by the state, by the government, by institutions of any sort. And that is our essence, and that essence is extremely powerful if we can protect that essence and allow it to voluntarily express itself into the world. It's the single most powerful force in human history.

> JAMES ELLIS (contemporary U.S. historian),
> in Ken Burns' "Thomas Jefferson"
> (television documentary), October 27, 2002

All religions must be tolerated for in this country every man must get to heaven his own way.

> FREDERICK II (Prussian king, 1712–1786)

The day that this country ceases to be free for irreligion, it will cease to be free for religion—except for the sect that can win political power.

> ROBERT H. JACKSON (U.S. Supreme Court
> associate justice, 1892–1954)

No man shall be compelled to frequent or support any religious worship, place, or ministry whatsoever, nor shall be enforced, restrained, molested, or burdened in his body or goods, nor shall otherwise suffer, on account of his religious opinions or belief; but that all men shall be free to profess, and by argument to maintain, their opinions in matters of religion, and that the same shall in no wise diminish, enlarge, or affect their civil capacities.

―――――

Believing with you that religion is a matter which lies solely between man and his God, that he owes account to none other for his faith or his worship, that the legislative powers of government reach action only, and not opinions, I contemplate with sovereign reverence that act of the whole American people which declares that their legislature should "make no law respecting an establishment of religion, or prohibiting the free exercise thereof," thus building a wall of separation between church and state.

THOMAS JEFFERSON (U.S. president, 1743–1826)

Religious freedom constitutes the very heart of human rights. Its inviolability is such that individuals must be recognized as having the right even to change their religion, if their conscience so demands.

JOHN PAUL II (contemporary Polish pope)

The first act of man, when he looked around and saw himself a creature which he did not make, and a world furnished for his reception, must have been devotion, and devotion must ever continue sacred to every individual man, as it appears right to him; and governments do mischief by interfering.

THOMAS PAINE (English-born U.S. political philosopher, 1737–1809)

Where the Spirit of the Lord is present, there is freedom.

PAUL (Christian apostle, first century A.D.), *2 Corinthians* 3:17

Nobody asks you of what religion you are, but if you can do the job.

ALEXIS de TOCQUEVILLE (French statesman and writer, 1805–1859), referring to the "extreme tolerance" he found, during his 1832 visit, among the settlers of Detroit ("a fine American village")

Everyone has the right to freedom of thought, conscience and religion; this right includes freedom to change his religion or belief, either alone or in community with others and in public or private, to manifest his religion or belief in teaching, practice, worship, and observance.

UNIVERSAL DECLARATION OF HUMAN RIGHTS,
United Nations, Article 18, 1948

I believe we are descendid from the Puritins, who nobly fled from a land of despitism to a land of freedim, where they could not only enjoy their own religion, but prevent everybody else from enjoyin *his.*

ARTEMUS WARD (U.S. writer and humorist, 1834–1867)

responsibility

Only through human freedom and responsibility are history and salvation able to fulfill themselves.

LEO BAECK (German theologian, 1873–1956)

The weight of the universe is pressed down on the shoulders of each moral agent to hold him to his task. The only path of escape known in all the worlds of God is performance. You must do your work, before you shall be released.

RALPH WALDO EMERSON (U.S. philosopher, 1803–1882)

Rights that do not flow directly from duty well performed are not worth having.

MOHANDAS K. GANDHI (Indian spiritual and nationalist leader, 1869–1948)

When the freedom they wished most for was freedom from responsibility, then Athens ceased to be free and was never free again.

EDITH HAMILTON (U.S. scholar and writer, 1865–1963)

Liberty not only means that the individual has both the opportunity and the burden of choice; it also means that he must bear the consequences of his actions. . . . Liberty and responsibility are inseparable.

F. A. HAYEK (Austrian-born British economist and philosopher, 1899–1992)

Responsibility is the price of freedom.

ELBERT HUBBARD (U.S. editor and writer, 1856–1915)

Take your life in your own hands, and what happens? A terrible thing: no one to blame.

ERICA JONG (contemporary U.S. writer)

I go for all sharing the privileges of the government, who assist in bearing its burdens.

ABRAHAM LINCOLN (U.S. president, 1809–1865)

[American liberty] is premised on the accountability of free men and women for what they have done, not for what they may do.

JON NEWMAN (contemporary U.S. lawyer and writer)

He who has been delivered from pain must not think he is now free again, and at liberty to take life up just as it was before, entirely forgetful of the past. He is now a "man whose eyes are open" with regard to pain and anguish, and he must help to overcome those two enemies (so far as human power can overcome them) and to bring the others the deliverance which he has himself enjoyed.

ALBERT SCHWEITZER (German physician and theologian, 1875–1965)

Liberty means responsibility. That's why most men dread it.

GEORGE BERNARD SHAW (British playwright and critic, 1856–1950)

The individual can never escape the moral burden of his existence. He must choose between obedience to authority and responsibility to himself. Moral decisions are often hard and painful to make. The temptation to delegate this burden to others is therefore ever-present. Yet, as all history teaches us, those who would take from man his moral burdens—be they priests or warlords, politicians or psychiatrists—must also take from him his liberty and hence his very humanity.

THOMAS S. SZASZ (contemporary
Hungarian-born U.S. psychiatrist)

Everyone has duties to the community in which alone the free and full development of his personality is possible.

UNIVERSAL DECLARATION OF HUMAN RIGHTS,
United Nations, Article 29, 1948

SELF-DISCIPLINE

Some people regard discipline as a chore. For me, it is a kind of order that sets me free to fly.

JULIE ANDREWS (contemporary
English-born U.S. actor)

Men are qualified for civil liberty in exact proportion to their disposition to put moral chains upon their own appetites. . . . Society cannot exist unless a controlling power upon will and appetite be placed somewhere; and the less of it there is within, the more there must be without. It is ordained in the eternal constitution of things that men of intemperate minds cannot be free. Their passions forge their fetters.

EDMUND BURKE (British statesman
and philosopher, 1729–1797)

Liberty is the right to discipline oneself in order not to be disciplined by others.

GEORGES CLEMENCEAU (French premier, 1841–1929)

Freedom stretches as far as your self-control.

MARIE von EBNER-ESCHENBACH
(Austrian writer, 1830–1916)

Liberty is the power we have over ourselves.

HUGO GROTIUS (Dutch scholar, 1583–1645)

The acceptance of boundaries and limits is the gateway to freedom.

PHIL JACKSON (contemporary U.S. basketball coach)

If we are to live our lives in peace and harmony, and if we are to achieve our ambitions of improving the conditions under which we live, we must have both freedom and discipline. **FOR FREEDOM WITHOUT DISCIPLINE IS ANARCHY; DISCIPLINE WITHOUT FREEDOM IS TYRANNY.**

JULIUS KAMBARAGE NYERERE
(Tanzanian president, 1922–1999)

To enjoy freedom,
if the platitude is
pardonable, we have
of course to control
ourselves. We must not
squander our powers,
helplessly and ignorantly,
squirting half the house
in order to water
a single rose-bush;
we must train them,
exactly and powerfully,
here on the very spot.

VIRGINIA WOOLF (English writer, 1882–1941)

SELF-REALIZATION

The way to final freedom is within thy Self.

THE BOOK OF THE GOLDEN PRECEPTS
(ancient Buddhist writing)

Our discontent begins by finding false villains whom we can accuse of deceiving us. Next we find false heroes whom we expect to liberate us. The hardest, most discomfiting discovery is that each of us must emancipate himself.

DANIEL J. BOORSTIN (contemporary U.S. historian)

There is probably no direct way to get in touch with our inner selves or to seek out satisfaction and happiness. It's best to live by sound principles—honesty, courage, liberty, and love—and then to await what unfolds. When, inevitably, we go astray for a time, we must return, once again, to living by the principles we cherish. The formula isn't all that difficult to understand; applying it is the work of a lifetime.

PETER R. BREGGIN (contemporary U.S. psychiatrist)

When one begins the transformative process, death and birth are imminent: the death of custom as authority, the birth of the self.

MARILYN FERGUSON (contemporary U.S. writer)

I want freedom for the full expression of my personality.

MOHANDAS K. GANDHI (Indian spiritual
and nationalist leader, 1869–1948)

HUMAN BEINGS HAVE AN INALIENABLE RIGHT TO INVENT THEMSELVES; WHEN THAT RIGHT IS PRE-EMPTED, IT IS CALLED BRAINWASHING.

GERMAINE GREER (contemporary Australian writer)

The true end of Man . . . is the highest and most harmonious development of his powers to a complete and consistent whole. Freedom is the first and indispensable condition which the possibility of such a development presupposes; but there is besides another essential—intimately connected with freedom, it is true—a variety of situations. Even the most free and self-reliant of men is hindered in his development, when set in a monotonous situation.

WILHELM von HUMBOLDT (German philologist
and diplomat, 1767–1835)

Man is always something more than what he knows of himself. He is not what he is simply once for all, but is a process; he is not merely an extant life, but is, within that life, endowed with possibilities through the freedom he possesses to make of himself what he will by the activities on which he decides.

KARL JASPERS (German psychiatrist
and philosopher, 1883–1969)

Personality is the supreme realization of the innate idiosyncrasy of a living being. It is an act of high greatest courage flung in the face of life, the absolute affirmation of all that constitutes the individual, the most successful adaptation to the universal conditions of existence coupled with the greatest possible freedom of self-determination.

CARL G. JUNG (Swiss psychiatrist, 1875–1961)

Our deepest fear is not that we are inadequate. Our deepest fear is that we are powerful beyond measure. It is our light, not our darkness, that most frightens us. We ask ourselves, who am I to be brilliant, gorgeous, talented and fabulous? Actually, who are you not to be? You are a child of God. Your playing small does not serve the world. There is nothing enlightened about shrinking so that other people won't feel insecure about you. We were born to make manifest the glory of God that is within us. It's not just in some of us; it's in everyone. And as we let our own light shine, we unconsciously give other people permission to do the same. As we are liberated from our own fear, our presence automatically liberates others.

MARRIANE WILLIAMSON (contemporary U.S. writer and lecturer)

IT IS ONLY BY THE BREAKING UP OF THE ESTABLISHED PATTERN THAT THE PROCESS OF INDIVIDUATION [I.E., SELF-REALIZATION] BECOMES POSSIBLE. On the other hand, individuation is not likely to come of itself. From the very outset anyone undertaking the experiment in depth is well advised to do everything in his power to bring into operation two great integrative factors: the fellowship of a working group; and the contact with the deep center.

———————

The good news is not primarily of hardship and of suffering, but of creative experience, an immense enlargement and enrichment of life. No aspect of the experiment in depth is more characteristic than this perceiving of everything, the inward world and the outward world alike, with eyes that, for the first time, see. That the way is hard is certain. But no less certain is its wonder. "Behold, I make all things new."

P. W. MARTIN (contemporary British psychologist), *Experiment in Depth*

**NO ONE CAN HELP US TO ACHIEVE THE INTI-
MATE ISOLATION BY WHICH WE FIND OUR
SECRET WORLDS, SO MYSTERIOUS, RICH AND
FULL. IF OTHERS INTERVENE, IT IS DESTROYED.**
This degree of thought, which we attain by freeing our-
selves from the external world, must be fed by the inner
spirit, and our surroundings cannot influence us in any
way other than to leave us in peace.

MARIA MONTESSORI (Italian physician
and educator, 1870–1952)

Withdrawal, detachment, simplification, reflection, liberation from automatism-these are all but preliminary
steps in the rebuilding of the self and the renewal of the
society of which we are a part. These initial acts may,
and in fact must, be taken by each of us alone: but the
purpose of our withdrawal, of our fasting and purgation,
is to reawaken our appetite for life, to make us keen to
discriminate between food and poison and ready to
exercise choice. Once we have taken the preparatory
steps, we must return to the group and reunite our-

selves with those who have been undergoing a like regeneration and are thereby capable of assuming responsibility and taking action. In relatively short order this fellowship may enfold men and women in every country, of every religious faith, of every cultural pattern.

LEWIS MUMFORD (U.S. sociologist, 1895–1990), *The Conduct of Life*

Integration means the creation of an inner unity, a center of strength and freedom, so that the being ceases to be a mere object, acted upon by outside forces, and becomes a subject, acting from its own "inner space" into the space outside itself.

E. F. SCHUMACHER (German-born British economist, 1911–1977), *A Guide for the Perplexed*

Simplicity and truth of character are not produced by the constraint of laws, nor by the authority of the state; no one the whole world over can be forced or legislated into a state of blessedness; the means required for such a consummation are faithful and brotherly admonition, sound education, and, above all, free use of the individual judgment.

BARUCH SPINOZA (Dutch philosopher, 1632–1677)

[Autonomy] is freedom to develop one's self—to increase one's knowledge, improve one's skills, and achieve responsibility for one's conduct. And it is freedom to lead one's own life, to choose among alternative courses of action so long as no injury to others results.

THOMAS S. SZASZ (contemporary
Hungarian-born U.S. psychiatrist)

I am always careful not to fall into the trap of "thinking I understand" just because I have had a glimmering of certain ideas which are quite plausible but which have not been part of my experience. . . .

The most important thing here is to *enter* into the experience, to feel that one is the material on which all sorts of relatively independent forces are acting. What allows me to be in a certain way the sculptor of myself, or at least to cooperate with the forces that shape me? If I don't do that, I am letting these forces operate and make whatever they wish of me. . . . Something in me is called on: as a human being, I am invited to take part in my own formation.

HENRI TRACOL (contemporary French
journalist and sculptor)

Now the real beginnings of the "freedom" which we have discussed for many years—and a heady freedom it is, coming after so many years of reaching outward for it—to finally discover all I had to do was reach inward, and it was there waiting all the time for me!

ALISA WELLS (contemporary U.S. photographer)

slavery

THE PRICE OF LIBERATION OF THE WHITE PEOPLE IS THE LIBERATION OF THE BLACKS—the total liberation, in the cities, in the towns, before the law, and in the mind.

JAMES BALDWIN (U.S. writer, 1924–1987)

A brave people will certainly prefer liberty, accompanied with a virtuous poverty, to a depraved and wealthy servitude.

EDMUND BURKE (British statesman and
philosopher, 1729–1797)

Neither slavery nor involuntary servitude, except as a punishment for crime whereof the party shall have been duly convicted, shall exist within the United States, or any place subject to their jurisdiction.

CONSTITUTION OF THE UNITED STATES,
Thirteenth Amendment, 1865

The right of the citizens of the United States to vote shall not be denied or abridged by the United States or by any State on account of race, color, or previous condition of servitude.

CONSTITUTION OF THE UNITED STATES,
Fifteenth Amendment, 1870

You can be up to your boobies in white satin, with gardenias in your hair and no sugar cane for miles, but you can still be working on a plantation.

BILLIE HOLIDAY (U.S. singer, 1915–1954)

How is it that we hear the loudest yelps for liberty among the drivers of Negroes?

SAMUEL JOHNSON (English writer and lexicographer, 1709–1784), referring, in 1775, to the Americans who were demanding independence from England

One hundred years of delay have passed since President Lincoln freed the slaves, yet their heirs, their grandsons, are not fully free. They are not yet freed from the bonds of injustice. They are not yet freed from social and economic oppression. And this nation, for all its hopes and all its boasts, will not be fully free until all its citizens are free.

JOHN F. KENNEDY (U.S. president, 1917–1963)

"I HAVE A DREAM" SPEECH

I have a dream that one day on the red hills of Georgia, sons of former slaves and sons of former slave-owners will be able to sit down together at the table of brotherhood.

I have a dream that one day, even the state of Mississippi, a state sweltering with the heat of injustice, sweltering with the heat of oppression, will be transformed into a oasis of freedom and justice.

I have a dream my four little children will one day live in a nation where they will not be judged by the color of their skin but by content of their character. I have a dream today! . . .

So let freedom ring from the prodigious hilltops of New Hampshire.

Let freedom ring from the mighty mountains of New York.

Let freedom ring from the heightening Alleghenies of Pennsylvania.

Let freedom ring from the snow-capped Rockies of Colorado.

Let freedom ring from the curvaceous slopes of California.

But not only that.

Let freedom ring from Stone Mountain of Georgia.

Let freedom ring from Lookout Mountain of Tennessee.

Let freedom ring from every hill and molehill of Mississippi, from every mountainside, let freedom ring.

And when we allow freedom to ring, when we let it ring from every village and hamlet, from every state and city, we will be able to speed up that day when all of God's children—black men and white men, Jews and Gentiles, Catholics and Protestants—will be able to join hands and to sing in the words of the old Negro spiritual, "Free at last, free at last; thank God Almighty, we are free at last."

MARTIN LUTHER KING JR. (U.S. clergyman
and human rights leader, 1929–1968)
Lincoln Memorial, Washington, D.C. August 28, 1963

I never will forget a moment in Birmingham when a white policeman accosted a little Negro girl seven or eight years old, who was walking in a demonstration with her mother. "What do you want?" the policemen asked her gruffly, and the little girl looked him straight in the eye and answered, "Fee-dom." She couldn't even pronounce it, but she knew. It was beautiful! Many times when I have been in sorely trying situations, the memory of that little one has come into my mind, and has buoyed me.

The Negro will only be truly free when he reaches down to the inner depths of his own being and signs with the pen and ink of assertive selfhood his own emancipation proclamation.

MARTIN LUTHER KING JR.

"A house divided against itself cannot stand." I believe this government cannot endure, permanently half slave and half free. I do not expect the Union to be dissolved—I do not expect the house to fall—but I do expect it will cease to be divided. It will become all one thing, or all the other.

This is a world of compensations; and he who would be no slave must consent to have no slave. Those who deny freedom to others, deserve it not for themselves; and, under a just God, cannot long retain it.

ABRAHAM LINCOLN (U.S. president, 1809–1865)

It is as difficult to make free a people that is resolved to live in slavery as it is to enslave a people that is determined to remain free.

NICCOLÒ MACHIAVELLI (Italian political
philosopher, 1469–1527)

I had no idea when I refused to give up my seat on that Montgomery bus [in 1955] that my small action would help put an end to the segregation laws in the south. I only knew that I was tired of being pushed around. I was a regular person, just as good as anybody else. There had been a few times in my life when I was treated by white people like a regular person, so I knew what that felt like. It was time. It was time that other white people started treating me that way.

ROSA PARKS (contemporary human rights activist). Parks was arrested for her civil disobedience and the next day Martin Luther King Jr. helped organize the Montgomery bus boycott, which marked the beginning of the modern civil rights movement. The boycott ended more than a year later when, on November 13, 1956, the U.S. Supreme Court ruled that segregation on public buses was unconstitutional.

Man was born free; and everywhere he is in chains. One thinks himself the master of others, and still remains a greater slave than they.

JEAN-JACQUES ROUSSEAU (French philosopher, 1712–1778)

Who can describe the injustice and the cruelties that in the course of centuries [the colored peoples of the world] have suffered at the hands of Europeans? . . .

We and our civilization are burdened, really, with a great debt. We are not free to confer benefits on these men, or not, as we please; it is our duty. Anything we give them is not benevolence but atonement.

ALBERT SCHWEITZER (German physician
and theologian, 1875–1965)

All government without the consent of the governed is the very definition of slavery.

JONATHAN SWIFT (Irish writer, 1667–1745)

Talk about slavery! It is not the peculiar institution of the South. It exists wherever men are bought and sold, wherever a man allows himself to be made a mere thing or a tool, and surrenders his inalienable rights of reason and conscience. Indeed, this slavery is more complete than that which enslaves the body alone.

HENRY DAVID THOREAU (U.S. philosopher, 1817–1862)

Oppression has, at one stroke, deprived the descendants of the Africans of almost all the privileges of humanity. The Negro of the United States has lost even the remembrance of his country; the language which his forefathers spoke is never heard around him; he abjured their religion and forgot their customs when he ceased to belong to Africa without acquiring any claim to European privileges.

ALEXIS de TOCQUEVILLE (French statesman and writer, 1805–1859)

When I found I had crossed dat line [to freedom], I looked at my hands to see if I was de same pusson. There was such a glory ober ebery ting; de sun came like gold through the trees, and ober the fields, and I felt like I was in Heaben.

HARRIET TUBMAN (U.S. emancipated slave and abolitionist), 1820–1913)

Oh, freedom! Oh, freedom
Oh, freedom over me!
Before I'll be a slave,
I'll be buried in my grave,
And go home to my Lord
And be free.

ANONYMOUS (AFRICAN-AMERICAN), "Oh, Freedom!"

social change

Every era of renaissance has come out of new freedoms for peoples. The coming renaissance will be greater than any in human history, for this time all the peoples of the earth will share in it.

PEARL BUCK (U.S. writer, 1892–1973)

CLAUDIA DREIFUS: I read somewhere that you are predicting that the twenty-first century, unlike the twentieth, is to be a century of peace and justice. Why?

DALAI LAMA: Because I believe that in the twentieth century, humanity has learned from many, many experiences. Some positive, and many negative. What misery, what destruction! The greatest number of human beings were killed in the two world wars of this century. But human nature is such that when we face a tremendous critical situation, the human mind can wake up and find some other alternative. That is a human capacity.

DALAI LAMA (contemporary Tibetan spiritual and temporal leader), 1997 interview

THERE ARE TWO SCHOOLS OF SOCIAL REFORM. One bases itself upon the notion of a morality which springs from an inner freedom, something mysteriously cooped up within personality. It asserts that the only way to change institutions is for men to purify their own hearts, and that when this has been accomplished, change of institutions will follow of itself. The other school denies the existence of any such inner power. . . . It says that men are made what they are by the forces of the environment, that human nature is purely malleable, and that till institutions are changed, nothing can be done. . . . There is an alternative to being penned in between these two theories. We can recognize that all conduct is interaction between elements of human nature and the environment, natural and social.

JOHN DEWEY (U.S. philosopher, 1859–1952)

Is there a spiritual reality, inconceivable to us today, which corresponds in history to the physical reality which Einstein discovered and which led to the atomic bomb? Einstein discovered a law of physical change: the way to convert a single particle of matter into enormous physical energy. Might there not also be, as Gandhi suggested, an equally incredible and [as yet]

undiscovered law of spiritual change, whereby a single person or small community of persons could be converted into an enormous spiritual energy capable of transforming a society and a world?

I BELIEVE THAT THERE IS, THAT THERE MUST BE, A SPIRITUAL REALITY CORRESPONDING TO $E=MC^2$ because from the standpoint of creative harmony, the universe is incomplete without it, and because, from the standpoint of moral freedom, humankind is sentenced to extinction without it.

JAMES W. DOUGLASS (contemporary U.S. human rights activist and writer)

What's wrong with this world is, it's not finished yet. It is not completed to that point where man can put his final signature to the job and say, "It is finished. We made it, and it works."

Because only man can complete it. Not God, but man. It is man's high destiny and proof of his immortality too, that his is the choice between ending the world, effacing it from the long annals of time and space, and completing it.

WILLIAM FAULKNER (U.S. writer, 1897–1962)

The history of the world is none other than the progress of the consciousness of freedom.

GEORG HEGEL (German philosopher, 1770–1831)

The "real movement" of history, it turns out, is fueled not by matter but by spirit, by the will to freedom.

GERTRUDE HIMMELFARB (contemporary U.S. historian)

The process of evolution can only be described as the gradual insertion of more and more freedom into matter.

T. E. HULME (English philosopher, 1883–1917)

Nothing is unchangeable but the inherent and inalienable rights of man.

THOMAS JEFFERSON (U.S. president, 1743–1826)

I refuse to accept the cynical notion that nation after nation must spiral down a militaristic stairway into the hell of thermonuclear destruction. I believe that unarmed truth and unconditional love will have the final word in reality. This is why right temporarily defeated is stronger than evil triumphant.

MARTIN LUTHER KING JR. (U.S. clergyman
and human rights leader, 1929–1968),
Nobel Peace Prize acceptance address,
Oslo, Norway, December 11, 1964

[The] transformation of man into an active, responsible individual is the new event which, more than any other, characterizes man. Of course the ancient mechanism of evolution, natural selection, will again enter into play. But, instead of depending as formerly on the slow action of biological laws and of chance, **NATURAL SELECTION NOW DEPENDS ON CONSCIENCE, A MANIFESTATION OF CEREBRAL ACTIVITY BASED ON FREEDOM** which becomes, in each of us, the means put at our disposal to advance.

PIERRE LECOMTE du NOÜY (French
biophysicist, 1883–1947)

At the earlier stages living organisms have had either no choice or very little choice about taking the new step. Progress was, in the main, something that happened to them, not something that they did. But the new step, the step from being creatures to being sons [and daughters] is voluntary. . . . It is voluntary in the sense that when it is offered to us we can refuse it. We can, if we please, shrink back; we can dig in our heels and let the new Humanity go on without us.

C. S. LEWIS (English writer, 1898–1963)

For collective action it suffices if the mass can be managed; collective growth is only possible through the freedom and enlargement of individual minds.

B. H. LIDDELL HART (English military
historian, 1895–1970)

The right of peaceable assembly and of petition . . . is the constitutional substitute for revolution.

ABRAHAM LINCOLN (U.S. president, 1809–1865)

Never doubt that a small group of thoughtful, committed people can change the world. Indeed, it's the only thing that ever does.

MARGARET MEAD (U.S. anthropologist, 1901–1978)

At moments of crisis, where the roads to disintegration or to development separate, as on a watershed, a single decisive personality, or a small group of informed and purposeful men, may by a slight push determine the direction and movement of an otherwise uncontrollable mass of conflicting social forces. At such moments not a single institution or group, but a whole society, will be involved in a change far beyond its ordinary capacities for adaptation: yet the dynamic agent in this transformation, the "spark which kindles the great forest," will be the individual human person; for it is he who precipitates the change in the social order by first initiating a profound regrouping of forces and ideal goals within himself. At such a moment the human integer represents the whole and in turn has an effect on the whole. **ONLY WITHIN THE COMPASS OF THE PERSON CAN A TOTAL CHANGE BE AFFECTED WITHIN THE SPAN OF A SINGLE GENERATION,** sufficient to produce the necessary effect on civilization at large: like the seed crystal, he passes on to the whole the new order of the part.

LEWIS MUMFORD (U.S. sociologist, 1895–1990)

Human history is the history of liberty, and liberty is history's golden thread.

MICHAEL NOVAK (contemporary U.S. writer)

Where, after all, do universal human rights begin? In small places, close to home—so close and so small that they cannot be seen on any map of the world. Yet they are the world of the individual person: the neighborhood he lives in; the school or college he attends; the factory, farm or office where he works. Such are the places where every man, woman and child seeks equal justice, equal opportunity, equal dignity without discrimination. Unless these rights have meaning there, they have little meaning anywhere. Without concerted citizen action to uphold them close to home, we shall look in vain for progress in the larger world.

ELEANOR ROOSEVELT (U.S. first lady and UN delegate, 1884–1962), United Nations address, March 27, 1958

The need for freedom of evolution is the sole basis of toleration, the sole valid argument against Inquisitions and Censorships, the sole reason for not burning heretics and sending every eccentric person to the madhouse.

GEORGE BERNARD SHAW (British
playwright and critic, 1856–1950)

All change in history, all advance, comes from the non-conformists. If there had been no troublemakers, no Dissenters, we should still be living in caves.

A. J. P. TAYLOR (English historian, 1906–1990)

A new and fair division of the goods and rights of this world should be the main object of those who conduct human affairs.

ALEXIS de TOCQUEVILLE (French statesman
and writer, 1805–1859)

THE RESPONSIBILITY FOR CHANGE . . . LIES WITH US. WE MUST BEGIN WITH OURSELVES, TEACHING OURSELVES NOT TO CLOSE OUR MINDS PREMATURELY TO THE NOVEL, THE SURPRISING, THE SEEMINGLY RADICAL. This means fighting off the idea-assassins who rush forward to kill any new suggestion on grounds of its impracticality, while defending whatever now exists as practical, no matter how absurd, oppressive, or unworkable it may be. It means fighting for freedom of expression—the right of people to voice their ideas, even if heretical.

Above all, it means starting this process of reconstruction now, before the further disintegration of existing political systems sends the forces of tyranny jack-booting through the streets, and makes impossible a peaceful transition to Twenty-first Century Democracy.

ALVIN TOFFLER (contemporary U.S. futurist)

We are now moving into a chapter of human history in which our choice is going to be, not between a whole world and a shredded-up world, but between one world and no world. I believe that the human race is going to choose life and good, not death and evil. I therefore believe in the imminence of one world, and I believe that, in the 21st century, human life is going to be a unity again in all its aspects and activities.

ARNOLD J. TOYNBEE (English historian, 1889–1975)

SPEECH
speech

YOU CAN CAGE THE SINGER
BUT NOT THE SONG.

HARRY BELAFONTE (contemporary
U.S. singer and actor)

Those who won our independence believed that the final end of the State was to make men free to develop their faculties. . . . They valued liberty both as an end and as a means. They believed liberty to be the secret of happiness and courage to be the secret of liberty. They believed that freedom to think as you will and to speak as you think are means indispensable to the discovery and spread of political truth; that without free speech and assembly discussion would be futile; that with them, discussion affords ordinarily adequate protection against the dissemination of noxious doctrine; that the greatest menace to freedom is an inert people; that public discussion is a political duty; and that this should be a fundamental principle of the American Government.

LOUIS D. BRANDEIS (U.S. Supreme Court
associate justice, 1856–1941)

If we don't believe in freedom of expression for people we despise, we don't believe in it at all.

NOAM CHOMSKY (contemporary U.S. linguist and political activist)

Though the whole world grumble, I will speak my mind.

CICERO (Roman statesman, first century B.C.)

The justification and the purpose of freedom of speech is not to indulge those who want to speak their minds. It is to prevent error and discover truth. There may be other ways of detecting error and discovering truth than that of free discussion, but so far we have not found them.

HENRY STEELE COMMAGER (U.S. historian, 1902–1998)

Congress shall make no law . . . abridging the freedom of speech.

CONSTITUTION OF THE UNITED STATES, Bill of Rights, First Amendment, 1791

They are trying to send us to prison for speaking our minds. Very well, let them. I tell you that if it had not been for men and women who in the past have had the moral courage to go to prison, we would still be in the jungles.

EUGENE V. DEBS (U.S. labor leader and presidential candidate, 1855–1926)

We who officially value freedom of speech above life itself seem to have nothing to talk about but the weather.

BARBARA EHRENREICH (contemporary U.S. writer)

Here in America we are descended in blood and in spirit from revolutionaries and rebels—men and women who dared to dissent from accepted doctrine. As their heirs, may we never confuse honest dissent with disloyal subversion.

DWIGHT D. EISENHOWER (U.S. president, 1890–1969)

I am aware that many object to the severity of my language [on the issue of slavery], but is there not cause for severity? I will be as harsh as truth, and as uncompromising as justice. On this subject, I do not wish to think, or speak, or write with moderation. No! No! Tell a man whose house is on fire, to give a moderate alarm; tell him to moderately rescue his wife from the hands of the ravisher; tell the mother to gradually extricate her babe from the fire into which it has fallen—but urge me not to use moderation in a cause like the present. I am in earnest—I will not equivocate—I will not excuse—I will not retreat a single inch; and I will be heard.

WILLIAM LLOYD GARRISON (U.S. editor
and abolitionist, 1805–1879)

The most stringent protection of free speech would not protect a man in falsely shouting fire in a theater and causing a panic. . . . The question in every case is whether the words used are used in such circumstances and are of such a nature as to create a clear and present danger that they will bring about the substantive evils that Congress has a right to prevent.

OLIVER WENDELL HOLMES JR. (U.S. Supreme Court
chief justice, 1841–1935)

The right to be heard does not automatically include the right to be taken seriously.

HUBERT H. HUMPHREY (Minnesota senator
and U.S. vice president, 1911–1978)

Timid men . . . prefer the calm of despotism to the boisterous sea of liberty.

THOMAS JEFFERSON (U.S. president, 1743–1826)

EVERY MAN HAS A RIGHT TO UTTER WHAT HE THINKS TRUTH, AND EVERY OTHER MAN HAS A RIGHT TO KNOCK HIM DOWN FOR IT.

SAMUEL JOHNSON (English writer and
lexicographer, 1709–1784)

The right to free speech is easily vitiated in the absence of an enforceable right to remain silent.

JOHN V. LINDSAY (New York City mayor, 1921–2000)

The Englishman's belief that his home is his castle and that the king cannot enter it, like the American's conviction that he must be able to look any man in the eye and tell him to go to hell, is the very essence of the free man's way of life.

WALTER LIPPMANN (U.S. journalist, 1889–1974)

EVERY FAMILY SHOULD EXTEND FIRST AMENDMENT RIGHTS TO ALL ITS MEMBERS, BUT THIS FREEDOM IS PARTICULARLY ESSENTIAL FOR OUR KIDS. Children must be able to say what they think, openly express their feelings, and ask for what they want and need if they are ever able to develop an integrated sense of self.

STEPHANIE MARSTON (contemporary
U.S. psychotherapist)

If all mankind minus one were of one opinion, mankind would be no more justified in silencing that one person than he, if he had the power, would be justified in silencing mankind.

———·———

To refuse a hearing to an opinion because they are sure that it is false, is to assume that their certainty is the same thing as absolute certainty. All silencing of discussion is an assumption of infallibility.

———·———

Though the silenced opinion be an error, it may, and very commonly does, contain a portion of truth; and since the general or prevailing opinion on any subject is rarely or never the whole truth, it is only by the collision of adverse opinions that the remainder of the truth has any chance of being supplied.

JOHN STUART MILL (English philosopher, 1806–1873)

GIVE ME THE LIBERTY TO KNOW, TO UTTER, AND TO ARGUE FREELY ACCORDING TO CONSCIENCE, ABOVE ALL LIBERTIES.

JOHN MILTON (English poet, 1608–1674), Areopagitica

If liberty means anything at all, it means the right to tell people what they do not want to hear.

GEORGE ORWELL (English writer, 1903–1950)

INSTEAD OF LOOKING ON DISCUSSION AS A STUMBLING BLOCK IN THE WAY OF ACTION, WE THINK IT AN INDISPENSABLE PRELIMINARY TO ANY WISE ACTION AT ALL.

PERICLES (Greek statesman, fifth century B.C.),
Funeral Oration, 431 B.C.

Free speech is the whole thing, the whole ball game. Free speech is life itself.

SALMAN RUSHDIE (contemporary
Indian-born British writer)

Does the restriction of money in campaigns deny anyone freedom of speech?

Of course it does. But we abridge free speech all the time, in protecting copyright, in ensuring defendants' rights to fair trials, in guarding privacy, in forbidding malicious defamation and incitement to riot. Because no single one of our rights is absolute, we restrain one when it treads too heavily on another.

That's why our courts have held repeatedly in the past century that the Constitution permits restrictions on political contributions. Just as antitrust laws encouraged competition in business, anti-contribution laws have enhanced competition in politics. **FREEDOM OF SPEECH IS DIMINISHED WHEN ONE VOICE WHO CAN AFFORD TO BUY THE TIME AND SPACE IS ALLOWED TO DROWN OUT THE OTHER SIDE.**

WILLIAM SAFIRE (contemporary U.S. journalist), referring
to a Senate bill introduced by John McCain and Russell
Feinberg limiting campaign contributions, 2001

THE EAGLE SUFFERS LITTLE BIRDS TO SING.

WILLIAM SHAKESPEARE (English playwright, 1564–1616), *Titus Andronicus*

When a man says he is Jesus or Napoléon, or that the Martians are after him, or claims something else that seems outrageous to common sense, he is labeled psychotic and locked up in the madhouse. Freedom of speech is only for normal people.

THOMAS S. SZASZ (contemporary Hungarian-born U.S. psychiatrist)

It is by the goodness of God that in our country we have those three unspeakably precious things: freedom of speech, freedom of conscience, and the prudence never to practice either of them.

MARK TWAIN (U.S. writer and humorist, 1835–1910)

I disapprove of what you
say, but I will defend to the
death your right to say it.

VOLTAIRE (French philosopher, 1694–1778)

THOUGHT AND OPINION

Every man haz a perfekt right tew hiz opinyun, provided it agrees with ours.

JOSH BILLINGS (U.S. writer and humorist, 1818–1885)

I may stand alone,
but would not change
my free thoughts for a throne.

LORD BYRON (English poet, 1788–1824), *Don Juan*

In a democratic system of thought control . . . [it is] necessary to take over the entire spectrum of opinion, the entire spectrum of discussion, so that nothing can be thinkable apart from the party line, not just that it be obeyed, but that you can't even think anything else. The state propaganda is not expressed; it's rather implicit; it's presupposed. It provides the framework for discussion among people who are . . . admitted into mainstream discussion.

NOAM CHOMSKY (contemporary U.S. linguist and political activist)

There is no such crime as a crime of thought; there are only crimes of action.

CLARENCE DARROW (U.S. lawyer, 1857–1938)

What is thought to be the responsible public opinion is, at any given time, a reflection of the needs and interests of the corporate technostructure.

JOHN KENNETH GALBRAITH (contemporary Canadian-born U.S. economist)

The most unpardonable sin in society is independence of thought.

EMMA GOLDMAN (Lithuanian-born U.S. political activist and writer, 1869–1940)

If there is any principle of the Constitution that more imperatively calls for attachment than any other, it is the principle of free thought—not free thought for those who agree with us but freedom for the thought that we hate.

OLIVER WENDELL HOLMES JR. (U.S. Supreme Court
chief justice, 1841–1935)

Those who begin coercive elimination of dissent soon find themselves exterminating dissenters. Compulsory unification of opinion achieves only the unanimity of the graveyard.

The priceless heritage of our society is the unrestricted constitutional right of each member to think as he will. Thought control is a copyright of totalitarianism, and we have no claim to it. It is not the function of our government to keep the citizen from falling into error; it is the function of the citizen to keep the government from falling into error.

ROBERT H. JACKSON (U.S. Supreme Court
associate justice, 1892–1954)

Subject opinion to coercion: whom will you make your inquisitors? Fallible men; men governed by bad passions, by private as well as public reasons. And why subject it to coercion? To produce uniformity. . . . Is uniformity attainable? Millions of innocent men, women, and children, since the introduction of Christianity, have been burnt, tortured, fined, imprisoned; yet we have not advanced one inch towards uniformity. **WHAT HAS BEEN THE EFFECT OF COERCION? TO MAKE ONE HALF THE WORLD FOOLS AND THE OTHER HALF HYPOCRITES.**

THOMAS JEFFERSON (U.S. president, 1743–1826)

The opinions of men are not the subject of civil government, nor under its jurisdiction. . . . It is time enough for the rightful purposes of civil government for its officers to interfere when principles break out into overt acts against peace and good order.

THOMAS JEFFERSON, The Virginia Act
for Religious Freedom, 1786

If there is anything that cannot bear free thought, let it crack.

WENDELL PHILLIPS (U.S. abolitionist and
social reformer, 1811–1884)

Thought is not free if the profession of certain opinions makes it impossible to earn a living. . . . Thought is not free if all the arguments on one side of a controversy are perpetually presented as attractively as possible, while the arguments on the other side can only be discovered by diligent search. . . .

Thought is free when it is exposed to free competition among beliefs, i.e., when all beliefs are able to state their case, and no legal or pecuniary advantages or disadvantages attach to beliefs.

BERTRAND RUSSELL (English mathematician
and philosopher, 1872–1970)

The most tyrannical governments are those which make crimes of opinions, for everyone has an inalienable right to his thoughts.

BARUCH SPINOZA (Dutch philosopher, 1632–1677)

Liberty of thought is the life of the soul.

VOLTAIRE (French philosopher, 1694–1778)

TRUTH AND KNOWLEDGE

Liberty cannot be preserved without a general knowledge among the people.

> JOHN ADAMS (U.S. president, 1735–1826)

The truth that makes men free is for the most part the truth which men prefer not to hear.

> HERBERT AGAR (U.S. journalist, 1897–1980)

Somebody has said that freedom of choice presupposes a full appreciation of all the alternatives involved, and one feature common to all propaganda is that it tries to limit our choice deliberately whether by avoiding argument (the bald statement of one point of view to the exclusion of others) or by the emotional and non-objective criticism of the other side and its opinions by the use of caricature, stereotype, and other means.

> J. A. C. BROWN (British psychiatrist, 1911–1964)

To choose, it is first necessary to know.

> HERMAN FINER (U.S. political scientist, 1898–1969)

If a nation expects to be ignorant and free . . . it expects what never was and never will be.

THOMAS JEFFERSON (U.S. president, 1743–1826)

You will know the truth, and the truth will make you free.

JESUS (Hebrew founder of Christianity,
first century A.D.), *John* 8:32

A popular government without popular information, or the means of acquiring it, is but a prologue to a farce or a tragedy; or, perhaps both. Knowledge will forever govern ignorance. And a people who mean to be their own governors must arm themselves with the power which knowledge gives.

JAMES MADISON (U.S. president, 1751–1836)

Let [truth] and falsehood grapple; who ever knew truth put to the worse in a free and open encounter?

JOHN MILTON (English poet, 1608–1674)

Such is the irresistible nature of truth that all it asks, and all it wants, is the liberty of appearing.

THOMAS PAINE (English-born U.S. political philosopher, 1737–1809)

I'm going to make a button: The truth will set you free, but first it will piss you off.

GLORIA STEINEM (contemporary U.S. women's rights leader and writer)

If we value the pursuit of knowledge, we must be free to follow wherever that search may lead us.

ADLAI E. STEVENSON (Illinois governor, presidential candidate, and UN ambassador, 1900–1965)

Those who talk about individuality the most are the ones who most object to deviation, and in a few years it may be the other way around. Some day everybody will think just what they want to think, and then everybody will probably be thinking alike.

ANDY WARHOL (U.S. artist, 1927–1987)

tyranny

As long as you keep a person down, some part of you has to be down there to hold him down, so it means you cannot soar as you otherwise might.

MARIAN ANDERSON (U.S. opera singer, 1902–1993)

THE COST OF LIBERTY IS LESS THAN THE PRICE OF REPRESSION.

W. E. B. DU BOIS (U.S. educator and writer, 1868–1963)

The moment a man says, "give up your rights, here is money," there is tyranny. It comes masquerading in monks' cowls, and in citizens' coats, comes savagely or comes politely. But it is tyranny.

RALPH WALDO EMERSON (U.S. philosopher, 1803–1882)

In South America euphemism appears to be the grisly preserve of violent power. "Liberty" was the name of the biggest prison in Uruguay under the military dictatorship, while in Chile one of the concentration camps was called "Dignity." It was the self-styled "Peace and Justice" paramilitary group in Chiapas [Mexico] that in 1997 shot 45 peasants in the back, nearly all of them women and children, as they prayed in a church. What have the souls of the south done over the past few decades to deserve quite so much liberty and dignity and peace and justice?

ISABEL FONSECA (contemporary U.S. journalist)

In their unrestrained eagerness to possess, the oppressors develop the conviction that it is possible for them to transform everything into objects of their purchasing power; hence their strictly materialistic concept of existence. Money is the measure of all things, and profit the primary goal . . . .

To the oppressor consciousness, the humanization of the "others," of the people, appears not as the pursuit of full humanity, but as subversion.

PAULO FREIRE (Brazilian educator, 1921–1997)

A STATE THAT DENIES ITS CITIZENS THEIR BASIC RIGHTS BECOMES A DANGER TO ITS NEIGHBORS AS WELL: internal arbitrary rule will be reflected in arbitrary external relations.

VÁCLAV HAVEL (contemporary Czech president)

The totalitarian brand of tyranny has perfected an awesome technique for stripping the individual of all material and spiritual resources which might bolster his independence and self-respect. It deprives him of every alternative and refuge—even that of silence or retreat into solitariness.

ERIC HOFFER (U.S. longshoreman
and philosopher, 1902–1983)

Every tyrant who ever lived has believed in freedom—for himself.

ELBERT HUBBARD (U.S. editor and writer, 1856–1915)

The Lord enters into judgment
   with the elders and princes of his people:
"It is you who have devoured the vineyard,
   the spoil of the poor is in your houses.
What do you mean by crushing my people,
   by grinding the face of the poor?"
says the Lord God of hosts.

ISAIAH (Hebrew prophet,
eighth century B.C.), *Isaiah* 3:14–15

Rebellion to tyrants is obedience to God.

THOMAS JEFFERSON (U.S. president,
1743–1826), motto on his seal

Can a nation be free if it oppresses other nations? It cannot.

VLADIMIR LENIN (Russian revolutionary
leader, 1870–1924)

The accumulation of all powers, legislative, executive, and judiciary, in the same hands, whether of one, a few, or many, and whether hereditary, self-appointed, or elective, may justly be pronounced the very definition of tyranny.

JAMES MADISON (U.S. president, 1751–1836)

I believe any man who takes the liberty of another into his keeping is bound to become a tyrant, and that any man who yields up his liberty, in however slight the measure, is bound to become a slave.

H. L. MENCKEN (U.S. journalist, 1880–1956)

Society . . . practices a social tyranny more formidable than many kinds of political oppression . . . penetrating much more deeply into the details of life, and enslaving the soul itself. Protection, therefore, against the tyranny of the magistrate is not enough: there needs protection also against the tyranny of the prevailing opinion and feeling; against the tendency of society to impose, by other means than civil penalties, its own ideas and practices as rules of conduct on those who dissent from them.

JOHN STUART MILL (English philosopher, 1806–1873)

Necessity is the plea for every infringement of human freedom. It is the argument of tyrants; it is the creed of slaves.

WILLIAM PITT the YOUNGER (English prime minister, 1759–1806)

What dictators call "internal unrest" . . . dissidents call "the spirit of human freedom."

> WILLIAM SAFIRE (contemporary U.S. journalist)

However sugarcoated and ambiguous, every form of authoritarianism must start with a belief in some group's greater right to power, whether that right is justified by sex, race, class, religion or all four. However far it may expand, the progression inevitably rests on unequal power and airtight roles within the family.

> GLORIA STEINEM (contemporary U.S. women's rights leader and writer)

The fundamental conflicts in human life are not between competing ideas—one of which is true and the other false, but rather, between those that hold power and use it to oppress others, and those who are oppressed by power and seek to free themselves of it.

> THOMAS S. SZASZ (contemporary Hungarian-born U.S. psychiatrist)

There is a natural and necessary progression from the extreme of anarchy to the extreme of tyranny; . . . arbitrary power is most easily established on the ruins of liberty abused to licentiousness.

GEORGE WASHINGTON (U.S. president, 1732–1799)

WOMEN
women

Do not put such unlimited power into the hands of the husbands. Remember all men would be tyrants if they could. If particular care is not paid to the ladies, we are determined to foment a rebellion, and will not hold ourselves bound by any laws in which we have no voice, no representation.

ABIGAIL ADAMS (U.S. first lady and writer, 1744–1818)

THE TRUE REPUBLIC: MEN, THEIR RIGHTS AND NOTHING MORE; WOMEN, THEIR RIGHTS AND NOTHING LESS.

SUSAN B. ANTHONY (U.S. women's rights leader, 1820–1906), motto of *Revolution* (feminist newspaper), 1868

We've got a generation now who were born with semi-equality. They don't know how it was before, so they think, this isn't too bad. We're working. We have our attaché cases and our three-piece suits. I get very disgusted with the younger generation of women. We had a torch to pass, and they are just sitting there. They don't realize it can be taken away. Things are going to have to get worse before they join in fighting the battle.

ERMA BOMBECK (U.S. writer and humorist, 1927–1996)

If the right of privacy means anything, it is the right of the individual, married or single, to be free from unwarranted governmental intrusion into matters so fundamentally affecting a person as the decision of whether to bear or beget a child.

WILLIAM J. BRENNAN JR. (U.S. Supreme Court associate justice, 1906–1997)

The right of citizens of the United States to vote shall not be denied or abridged by the United States or by any State on account of sex.

CONSTITUTION OF THE UNITED STATES, Nineteen Amendment, 1920

The embattled gates to equal rights indeed opened up for modern women, but I sometimes think to myself: That is not what I meant by freedom—it is only "social progress."

HELENE DEUTSCH (Polish-born U.S. psychoanalyst, 1884–1982)

WHEN A GREAT TRUTH ONCE GETS ABROAD IN THE WORLD, NO POWER ON EARTH CAN IMPRISON IT, OR PRESCRIBE ITS LIMITS, OR SUPPRESS IT. It is bound to go on till it becomes the thought of the world. Such a truth is woman's right to equal liberty with man. She was born with it. It was hers before she comprehended it. It is prescribed upon all the powers and faculties of her soul, and no custom, law nor usage can ever destroy it.

FREDERICK DOUGLASS (U.S. escaped slave, abolitionist, and social reformer, 1817–1895)

Legislation to apply the principle of equal pay for equal work without discrimination because of sex is a matter of simple justice.

DWIGHT D. EISENHOWER (U.S. president, 1890–1969), State of the Union Message, January 5, 1956

Let the laws be purged of every barbarous remainder, every barbarous impediment to women.

RALPH WALDO EMERSON (U.S. philosopher, 1803–1882)

Equality of rights under the law shall not be denied or abridged by the United States or by any State on account of sex.

EQUAL RIGHTS AMENDMENT (a proposed constitutional amendment which was defeated in 1982)

[Feminism] asks that women be free to define them-selves—instead of having their identity defined for them, time and again, by their culture and their men.

SUSAN FALUDI (contemporary U.S. writer)

It is easier to live through someone else than to com-plete yourself. The freedom to lead and plan your own life is frightening if you have never faced it before. It is frightening when a woman finally realizes that there is no answer to the question "who am I" except the voice inside herself.

BETTY FRIEDAN (contemporary U.S. women's rights leader and writer), *The Feminine Mystique*

[A woman's right to choose an abortion is] something central to a woman's life, to her dignity. . . . And when government controls that decision for her, she's being treated as less than a full adult human being responsible for her own choices.

RUTH BADER GINSBERG (contemporary
U.S. Supreme Court associate justice)

The right to vote, or equal civil rights, may be good demands, but **TRUE EMANCIPATION BEGINS NEITHER AT THE POLLS NOR IN THE COURTS. IT BEGINS IN WOMAN'S SOUL.**

EMMA GOLDMAN (Lithuanian-born U.S.
political activist and writer, 1869–1940)

Woman is born free and her rights are the same as those of a man. . . . All citizens, be they men or women, being equal in [the state's] eyes, must be equally eligible for all public offices, positions and jobs, according to their capacity and without any other criteria than those of their virtues and talents.

OLYMPE de GOUGES (French writer, 1748–1793),
referring to Article 1 of the Declaration of the
Rights of Man and the Citizen, 1789

Women's liberation is the liberation of the feminine in the man and the masculine in the woman.

CORITA KENT (U.S. graphic artist, 1918–1986)

It is capitalist America that produced the modern independent woman. Never in history have women had more freedom of choice in regard to dress, behavior, career, and sexual orientation.

CAMILLE PAGLIA (contemporary U.S. writer)

FOR ME, TO BE A FEMINIST IS TO ANSWER THE QUESTION: "ARE WOMEN HUMAN?" WITH A YES. It is not about whether women are better than, worse than or identical with men. It's certainly not about trading personal liberty—abortion, divorce, sexual self-expression—for social protection as wives and mothers, as pro-life feminists propose. It's about justice, fairness and access to the broad range of human experience. It's about women consulting their own well-being and being judged as individuals rather than as members of a class with one personality, one social function, one road to happiness. It's about women having intrinsic value as persons rather than contingent value as a means to an end for others: fetuses, children, "the family," men.

KATHA POLLITT (contemporary U.S. journalist and poet)

Woman must not accept; she must challenge. She must not be awed by that which has been built up around her; she must reverence that within her which struggles for expression. Her eyes must be less upon what is and more clearly upon what should be. She must listen only with a frankly questioning attitude to the dogmatized opinions of man-made society. When she chooses the new, free course of action, it must be in the light of her own opinion—of her own intuition. Only so can she give play to the feminine spirit. Only thus can she free her mate from the bondage which he wrought for himself when he wrought hers. Only thus can she restore to him that of which he robbed himself in restricting her. Only thus can she remake the world.

MARGARET SANGER (U.S. women's rights leader and writer, 1879–1966)

Can man be free if woman be a slave?

PERCY BYSSHE SHELLEY (English poet, 1792–1822)

Just think—guns have a constitutional amendment protecting them and women don't.

ELEANOR SMEAL (contemporary women's rights leader)

WE HOLD THESE TRUTHS TO BE SELF-
EVIDENT: THAT ALL MEN AND WOMEN
ARE CREATED EQUAL; THAT THEY ARE
ENDOWED BY THEIR CREATOR WITH
CERTAIN ALIENABLE RIGHTS; THAT
AMONG THESE ARE LIFE, LIBERTY, AND
THE PURSUIT OF HAPPINESS.

ELIZABETH CADY STANTON (U.S. women's
rights leader and writer, 1815–1892),
"Declaration of Sentiments", July 19, 1848

index of authors

acknowledgments

I acknowledge with pleasure and gratitude the friends who assisted me and gave me moral support while editing this book: Wade Hudson, Elizabeth Pomada and Michael Larsen (my literary agents), Robert Arbegast, Rosalie Maggio, and Jena Pincott and Tom Russell (my Random House editors). Jena came up with the original idea for the book. Thank you, thank you all very much!